The Sophisticated Sandwich

Other books in the Aris *Kitchen Edition* series:

Grain Gastronomy by Janet Fletcher

Antipasto Feasts by Karen A. Lucas and Lisa Wilson

Peppers Hot and Chile by Georgeanne Brennan and
Charlotte Glenn

Glories of the Vegetarian Table by Janet Hazen

The Sophisticated Sandwich

**Exotic,
Eclectic,
Ethnic
Eatables**

Janet Hazen

Kitchen Edition
Aris Books

Addison-Wesley Publishing Company, Inc.
Reading, Massachusetts   Menlo Park, California   New York
Don Mills, Ontario   Wokingham, England   Amsterdam   Bonn
Sydney   Singapore   Tokyo   Madrid   San Juan

Many of the designations used by manufacturers and sellers to distinguish their products are claimed as trademarks. Where those designations appear in this book and Addison-Wesley was aware of a trademark claim, the designations have been printed in initial capital letters (e.g., Velveeta).

Library of Congress Cataloging-in-Publication Data

Hazen, Janet.
    The sophisticated sandwich: exotic, eclectic, ethnic eatables /
Janet Hazen.
        p. cm. — (Kitchen edition)
    Includes index.
    ISBN 0-201-19625-5
    1. Sandwiches. I. Title. II. Series.
TX818.H39 1989
641.8′4—dc19

88-34908
CIP

Kitchen Edition books are published by Aris Books,
an imprint of Addison-Wesley Publishing Company, Inc.

Aris Books Editorial Offices and
Test Kitchen
1621 Fifth Street
Berkeley, CA 94710
(415) 527-5171

Series Editor: John Harris
Book Designer: Jenny Kilgore
Cover Photographer: Lisa Blevins
Cover Designer: Copenhaver Cumpston
Food Stylist: Stevie Bass
Illustrator: Pamela Manley

Set in 10.5 point Times Roman by Another Point, Inc., Oakland, CA

ABCDEFGHIJ-DO-89
First printing, May 1989

This book is dedicated to all the cooks and chefs who create magnificent works of art on a regular basis, but who receive little or no attention for their love, devotion, and skill.

Thank you, Gilles, for love, support, and lots of answers!

Contents

Introduction

The Earl of Sandwich has quite a following. The familiar sandwich story goes like this: John Montagu, the fourth Earl of Sandwich, was sitting at the card table intent on the game and, needless to say, winning. As fate would have it, hunger reared its ugly head and the Earl demanded a snack. He needed something to eat out of his hand so that he could concentrate on the cards, not on a knife and fork. An even worse fate would have been being forced to leave the playing table. A savvy servant brought a piece of meat between two pieces of bread, and the sandwich was invented. Somehow the thought of this "sandwich" brings to mind a large leg of something, bone and all, wedged between two stale, crusty pieces of dry bread. Maybe I am wrong. But at any rate, if this is a true account, I think the sandwich should have been named after the servant.

Naturally there are contenders for the honor of originating the sandwich. Ancient Babylon is the setting for the tale that a rabbi first placed some bitter herbs between two slices of unleavened bread to symbolize Jewish privations in Egypt. Let us not forget the "trencher," a round piece of bread used as a plate for hot and cold food. Apparently only the poor ate the bread, which was usually soaked in gravy by the end of the meal. The trencher is also said to predate the rudimentary sandwich served to the Earl of Sandwich. Culinary history is interesting, but what really matters is not who invented the sandwich or how, but that it *was* invented. As with most great discoveries, many countries and even more individuals take claim for the original goods.

What is an American sandwich? Our culinary history has been influenced by so many international cuisines that what we consider an American sandwich was most likely "brought over" on the proverbial *Boat*. I believe that not too many years from now Asian food will be a staple of American cuisine. We cannot help but embrace new, exotic, and foreign foodstuffs, cooking methods, and ideas. American culture is a patchwork of many cultures and so is our culinary history.

Sandwiches presented a big challenge to the homemaker of the fifties, and entire cookbooks were devoted to the subject. Ingredients, style, and presentation have come a long way since 1952, but those times set the ground for innovative and unique sandwiches. Novice and professional cooks strove to create new and different recipes for sandwiches. My mom showed me a late 1950s magazine article with a two-page spread on sandwiches. All the recipes are written in a very casual tone, but my favorite is Shrimp Salad Sandwich: "Chop up some drained canned shrimp. Add finely chopped cucumber (unpeeled, please) and onion. Stir in a little mayonnaise, a dribble of salad oil, a few drops of vinegar, a touch of tarragon, salt, and pepper. Spread on thin rye bread and serve with raw carrots and olives." The sandwich is pictured with a tall glass of iced tea and a cup of milk. Sandwiches have come a long way.

Almost every cuisine has a typical sandwich. No, Americans cannot claim this as a first, either. Examples of international sandwiches abound: Filled Mexican tortillas (see Open-Face Sandwiches), Chinese pork buns, El Salvadoran papusas and tamales, Middle Eastern pitas (see Warm and Melted Sandwiches), English tea sandwiches, and French Croque Monsieur, Croque Vivienne, and Croque Madam (see Grilled Sandwiches). Italians have been enjoying Panini for centuries (see Pan Bagna, Room-Temperature Sandwiches). Countless others haven't made their way into culinary history books. The Danish are perhaps most famous for their Smørrebrød, sandwiches that began as pieces of hearty bread spread with grease, fat, or butter. "To butter" translates "to grease" in Danish. "Palaeg" means "something laid on," a concept that added an ingredient to the butter-spread bread. Smørrebrød is almost always open-faced and can be any combination of bread, usually rye, a spread, and meat, poultry, fish, or cheese. Many shops in Denmark sell a wide variety of made-up sandwiches. This food "group" is a staple in Denmark. Sandwiches comprise one of the most popular concepts around the world and can be found anywhere and everywhere.

Up-scale restaurants are starting to bring back classic sandwiches, some with a new twist, others in their original form. Let's face it: certain recipes need no improvement. Original and unique creations are also appearing on many menus. Granted, there are still some pretty boring, poorly constructed examples of the sandwich. But within the American culinary awakening bright chefs and cooks are creating wonderful food. Sandwiches are still the preferred lunchtime meal for most of America.

The sandwich may have been born with bread, but no law requires it to continue its entire life that way. "Sandwich" means "to sandwich" between two pieces of "something." All sandwiches do not have to follow this prescribed definition.

Sandwich-making standards are high. The rules and boundaries are flexible, but the judging is strict! Some basic guidelines must be followed for successful results. A sandwich is good if it has a pleasing taste—this is obvious. There are, however, some important factors besides taste. In a winning sandwich, each component should be good if eaten alone, but somehow combining many ingredients makes for dazzling results. Textures can vary within one bite—this tickles and delights the palate. Colors can be contrasting and bright or subtle and monochromatic. The bread or other carrier must perform its task with style.

If a sandwich is too difficult to eat with the hands, it must be delegated to the open-face category. Carriers must always be fresh and wholesome. If the sandwich bread is supposed to be oil soaked, don't expect a crispy, crusty holder. Generally speaking, the bread must be protected from wet or soggy ingredients. A thin layer of mayonnaise will not achieve this goal. I usually like to place some sort of green between the bread and the other ingredients. A bright green or red leaf next to the rather neutral-colored bread is attractive and adds contrast in texture as well as color and taste. All in all, the sandwich must be a treat for the eye as well as the taste buds.

The sandwiches presented in this book come in every shape and form possible.The Open-Face section challenges the very definition of the sandwich with its use of non-bread holders. Many must be eaten on a plate with a fork and knife. Sandwiches can be layered, stacked, sliced, rolled, quartered, fried, baked, grilled, griddled, steamed, served hot or at room temperature. They are versatile, to say the least.

The recipes in this book will brighten any stale attitudes about the boring state of the sandwich. All but a few are my own creations. When recipes were tested and tasted, I got comments like, "What a good idea. I never would have thought of this combination" time and time again. I hope this volume will serve as inspiration as well as a recipe book.

Basics

Basic Techniques

TO ROAST PEPPERS

Hold a fresh pepper over an open flame or grill over red-hot charcoal. Rotate the pepper until all sides are blackened evenly. Place the charred pepper in a plastic bag and seal. Steam the pepper for one hour. Remove it from the bag and peel the pepper under running water. Remove the seeds and stem. Peppers can also be roasted in a 500° F oven; place the peppers on a heavy cookie sheet, place in hot oven, and rotate as the skin begins to turn black. Follow the remaining steps for steaming and peeling.

TO CLARIFY BUTTER

Melt the butter in a heavy saucepan. When it has melted completely, skim the foam off the surface and discard. Carefully pour the butter into a container, leaving the milky solids behind. Refrigerate the clarified butter, covered, for up to one month. A pound and a quarter of raw butter makes about one pound of clarified butter.

MARINATING

Marinating provides three services: it tenderizes, adds flavor, and coats food with oil and other liquids, which aids in the cooking process. Generally speaking, light flavors require a light marinade and assertive flavors call for an assertive marinade.

A successful marinade has three elements: acid, oil, and flavoring agent. The acid can be wine, vinegar, citrus juices, or tomato. Any good oil can be used as long as it complements the flavors of the entire dish or meal. A full-flavored oil such as sesame or a fruity olive oil can be used for this purpose. The flavoring agent can be herbs, spices, mustards, or condiments. I often prefer a complex marinade, which of course adds complexity to the final product, although simple marinades can be effective, too.

ROASTING MEAT

Roasting, a dry-heat method of cooking, requires a rack and a roasting pan large enough to catch the juices and fats that drip from the food. Usually herbs, spices, and some kind of fat are rubbed into the food before roasting. Many recipes call for salt, but I never use salt during the roasting process. Some people believe that salt draws the juices out of food as it cooks. Salt can be added later.

The food should be at room temperature before roasting begins. Place the prepared food on the rack and lay it across or in the greased pan. Place in a hot oven (450°–500° F). Roast at high heat for 5 minutes, to seal in the juices. Immediately reduce the heat to the prescribed temperature and continue to cook until done. Remember that food continues to cook for a short while after it is removed from the oven. Allow it to rest for at least 10 minutes before cutting, to allow the juices to be drawn back into the food.

Do not test food by inserting a fork or tester into meat; this allows the juices to escape, leaving the food dry and lessening flavor. You may of course use a thermometer, or adhere to the time given in the recipe.

GRILLING

Grilling refers to cooking on a metal grill over hot coals. Many good books on grilling are available, and I won't attempt to compete with them. A few basic concepts are important, however.

1. Food should be at room temperature before cooking.
2. Food should have a coating of oil.
3. Grill should be clean and coals hot and spread evenly.
4. Remove food from the grill promptly. Remember, food retains heat and continues cooking after it is removed from the heat source.
5. Try not to handle delicate foods too much as they will break apart.
6. Food often sticks to the grill if you try to turn the first side before it is done.
7. Scoring or making a cross-hatch design on food makes for an attractive presentation. This takes practice, but the results are worth it.

GRIDDLE COOKING

There is confusion about the difference between griddle cooking and grilling. Many restaurants and chefs use these terms interchangeably. Griddle cooking or griddling is done on a flat surface known as a griddle. Greasy spoons use the griddle for almost everything! Since most of us don't have griddles at home, we must use a frying pan or skillet. I prefer nonstick varieties, but cast iron works very well for this type of cooking.

Heat the fat in a skillet. Place the food in the pan and reduce the heat to low. Cheese that must be melted requires longer cooking on low heat. It is too easy to brown bread and leave the interior of a sandwich cold, uncooked, or unmelted. Placing a cover on the skillet helps to melt cheese and heat the interior without overcooking the bread or exterior. Always be sure you have enough oil or butter left when the sandwich is flipped, because bread absorbs quite a bit of fat. I suggest using oil or clarified butter for griddle cooking. Raw butter burns quickly and blackens the bread, once again, without heating the inside. Sandwich ingredients, such as meats, fish, and poultry must be fully cooked before being finished on a griddle.

Basic Tips

1. Always read an entire recipe at least twice before you begin shopping or cooking.

2. Add additional salt, pepper, herbs, or spices after you have tasted the dish.

3. Use a cover while griddle-cooking sandwiches, to melt cheese and heat the interior of the sandwich.

4. Buy sun-dried tomatoes in bulk instead of the oil-packed variety. Reconstitute the tomatoes by soaking them in boiling water until they are soft, about 5 to 20 minutes.

5. Most recipes in this book can be halved or doubled successfully.

6. Food continues to cook for 5 to 10 minutes after it is removed from the heat source.

7. Nonreactive pots and pans refer to metals that do not interact with certain foods, usually acids. Copper and aluminum should be avoided when cooking with such acidic foods as tomatoes and vinegar. Nearly every other cooking surface is considered non-reactive.

Basic Recipes

Mustards

There are many good mustards on the market. Shoppers can choose from traditional German, Dijon, Chinese hot, and French tarragon to the more exotic California honey mustard, to name just a few. A modest pantry should include at least four quality mustards. Choose a full-flavored robust variety, hot/sweet, spicy-hot, Dijon, one coarse-grained type, and perhaps an herbed French mustard. These should satisfy most sandwich needs.

I have provided some easy recipes for those of you who would like to make your own mustard. All of them are listed as ingredients throughout this book and can be used as described in each recipe or as you wish. I'm sure you could impress your friends with homemade bread, mayonnaise, and mustard all for one meal!

Hot-Pepper Coarse-Grained Mustard

For those who love hot and spicy food, this mustard is guaranteed to bring tears to the eyes. It is very tasty and can be used with discretion for "normal" palates. This mustard is excellent with smoked meats and assertive cheeses. Use it with Sardines and Canadian Bacon with Egg on Toasted Whole Wheat Bread (see page 51) or Baked Ham, Tilsit, and Dill Pickle on Black Bread (see page 74).

⅓ cup yellow mustard seeds
3 dried small red peppers
2 Tb. dry mustard
2 Tb. apple cider vinegar
2 Tb. water
3 Tb. olive oil
¼ cup soy sauce
1 tsp. turmeric
1 clove garlic
Salt, to taste

Place the ingredients in a food processor and process until the mixture is a coarse paste. Taste and adjust the seasoning. Allow the mustard to sit at room temperature, covered, for 4 hours before using. Mustard improves with age and may be stored in the refrigerator for several months.

Makes about 1½ cups.

Tomato-Herb Mustard

The tomato makes this robust mustard almost light and fluffy, and the herbed vinegar and dried herbs add an unusual flavor to it. I have chosen this mustard to go with Grilled Sausage with Pepper-Onion Sauté on Italian Roll (see page 78), Grilled Cheddar and Turkey with Sweet Pickles and Tomato on Oatmeal Bread (see page 85), and Croque Monsieur (see page 94).

Soak the seeds in the vinegar, water, and olive oil for 8 hours or overnight.

In a food processor, process the seeds with the soaking liquid, garlic, herbs, tomato, and salt to a smooth paste. Taste and adjust for salt and pepper. May be stored in the refrigerator for several months.

Makes about 1 cup.

⅓ cup yellow mustard seeds
¼ cup herbed red wine vinegar
1 Tb. water
1 Tb. olive oil
2 cloves garlic
1 tsp. each basil, tarragon, and chervil
1 small tomato, chopped
1 tsp. salt
Pepper, to taste

Honey Mustard

A tangy mustard, slightly sweet, thick, and golden, makes a great marinade for chicken or meat. Simply rub the mustard on chicken or meat and coat with chopped nuts. Roast, bake, or fry as usual. Serve with Roast Lamb with Fried Garlic on Rosemary Fougasse (see page 53) and Sardines, Onion, and Mustard Greens on Toasted Black Bread (see page 67).

Combine the ingredients in a small bowl and mix to a smooth paste. Allow the mustard to sit at room temperature, covered, for 4 hours before using. May be stored in the refrigerator for several months.

Makes about ½ cup.

⅓ cup dry mustard
1 Tb. sherry vinegar
3 Tb. honey
½ tsp. salt

Horseradish Mustard

This very pungent mustard is made even hotter by the addition of horseradish. Use it judiciously with Fried Oysters and Corn-Pepper Tartar Sauce on Warm French Bread (see page 70) and Reuben Sandwich (see page 89).

½ cup yellow mustard seeds
1 Tb. dry mustard
¼ cup seasoned rice wine vinegar
¼ cup water
2 Tb. horseradish
½ tsp. salt

Soak the mustard seeds and dry mustard in the vinegar and water for 8 hours or overnight.

Add the horseradish and salt to the soaked mustard seeds. In a food processor, process to a smooth paste. Taste and adjust for salt. May be stored in the refrigerator for several months.

Makes about 1½ cups.

Mayonnaise

There is a big difference between store-bought and homemade mayonnaise. If you have never made it yourself, try it once to see the difference. Most folks prefer it. The homemade variety takes just a couple of minutes to throw together in a blender and keeps for about 2 weeks in the refrigerator.

2 large egg yolks
1 clove garlic
1½ Tb. Dijon mustard
Juice of 1 lemon
1 cup vegetable oil
½ cup olive oil
1 Tb. white wine or Champagne vinegar
Salt and pepper, to taste

Place the egg yolks, garlic, mustard, and lemon juice in a blender. Blend for 30 seconds. With the motor running, slowly add the vegetable oil in a thin stream. Mixture should start to form an emulsion. When the mixture gets thick, you may add the oil in a thicker stream. Add the olive oil, vinegar, salt, and pepper. Taste and adjust the seasoning. The mayonnaise should be thick and smooth and will keep refrigerated up to 2 weeks.

If the mayonnaise should break (oil separates from eggs), simply remove from the blender and place in a bowl. Whisk the mixture into another bowl, slowly, allowing an emulsion to form.

Makes about 2 cups.

Fresh Tomato Sauce

*T*his tomato sauce is fast and easy to prepare. It is delicious with fresh pasta and is perfect anytime an abundance of fresh tomatoes is available. Use for Grilled Polenta and Vegetable Ricotta Filling with Pancetta Tomato Sauce (see page 90).

Cook the onions, garlic, and herbs in the olive oil over moderate heat until soft, about 20 minutes. Add the chopped tomatoes and cook over high heat for 5 minutes. Reduce the heat and cook over moderate heat for 30 to 40 minutes or until the tomatoes are soft and the mixture is thick.

Transfer to a blender and purée to a smooth sauce. Strain the sauce through a fine wire mesh to remove the skins and seeds. Return the sauce to the pan and cook over low heat for 10 minutes. Season with salt and pepper.

Makes 4 to 6 cups.

2 medium onions, medium dice
4 cloves garlic, minced
1 tsp. each dry marjoram, oregano, and basil
⅓ cup olive oil
3 pounds fresh (about 15–17) tomatoes, chopped
Salt and pepper, to taste

Canned-Tomato Sauce

*U*nfortunately, fresh tomatoes are not available year round. However, canned tomatoes are not a bad substitute. The addition of a bit of sugar takes away some of the acid flavor found in canned tomatoes. This sauce is chunkier than that made with fresh tomatoes.

Cook the onions, garlic, and herbs in olive oil over moderate heat until soft, about 20 minutes. Add the red wine and cook over high heat until it evaporates. Add the tomatoes and cook over high heat for 5 minutes. Reduce the heat and cook slowly for 15 to 20 minutes. Cool slightly. Purée in a blender. Return the sauce to the pan and cook for 10 minutes. Add the sugar, salt, and pepper.

Makes 4 to 6 cups.

2 yellow onions, chopped
4 cloves garlic, minced
1 tsp. each marjoram, oregano, and basil
½ cup olive oil
Splash red wine
2 (28-ounce) cans chopped tomatoes
2 tsp. sugar
Salt and pepper, to taste

Chinese Five-Spice Powder

If you cannot locate this spice mix in a specialty or Asian food shop, you can make it from scratch. It's a fragrant and heady mixture of spices for poultry, fish, and meat.

1½ Tb. Szechuan
    peppercorns
1 Tb. fennel seeds
4 star anise
1 1-inch stick cinnamon
2 tsp. coriander seeds

Grind all the spices to a fine powder. Store the mix in an airtight container.

Five-Pepper Mix

2 Tb. red peppercorns
2 Tb. green peppercorns
2 Tb. white peppercorns
2 Tb. black peppercorns
1 Tb. allspice

Grind to a fine powder and store in a tightly closed bottle.

Basic Polenta

6 cups water
2 cloves garlic, minced
4 Tb. unsalted butter
2 cups coarse yellow
    cornmeal
Salt and pepper, to taste

Place the water, garlic, and butter in a large heavy-bottom saucepan. Bring the water to a boil. Slowly add the cornmeal, whisking all the while. When all the cornmeal has been added, reduce the heat and cook over moderate heat for 20 to 25 minutes or until the cornmeal is soft and not grainy. You may add up to ½ cup more water if the polenta is too thick. Stir the polenta constantly for the first 5 minutes and frequently thereafter. Season with salt and pepper.
    Makes 6 to 8 servings.

Bread Recipes

At an early age I realized that the joy of food was found not just in the eating but in the cooking as well. The art of preparing culinary treats was a comfortable one. I am a painter and sculptor, so the *art* of cooking came naturally to me. It brings me great pleasure and is full of surprises and offers plenty of opportunities for creativity. Alas, as soon as I had been seduced by cooking, an irrational fear of baking possessed me. The thought of weighing ingredients and using a scale or a measuring cup, much less a thermometer, was intimidating. Running around the kitchen with a stopwatch around my neck, shutting windows, and maintaining the perfect rising temperature was not my idea of fun. Reading recipes that contained the dreaded word *yeast* was enough to scare me off. I would quickly turn the page and forget that such a loathsome idea existed. As you may imagine, I never developed much of a feel for baking.

Luckily, I have generous friends and family who not only adore the sport but do exceedingly well at it. They have created some of the most exciting, innovative, and plain ol' delicious breads for this sandwich book. Bread recipes were designed for the fillings of each particular sandwich. A word of advice—just because the breads are part of a sandwich recipe doesn't mean they *need* other flavors to help them along or disguise plain or average qualities.

All these breads make great eating with butter, jam, olive oil, peanut butter, or just plain. In most cases the yield for each bread recipe will leave you plenty of leftovers, to be quickly devoured once your family and friends get hold of them.

Trust me on this count: None of these recipes is difficult or tricky. When I gather the courage to bake a single item I am usually surprised by the simplicity and forgiveness of the bread dough. Imagine bread dough and *yeast* being forgiving. The truth is that all those notions about thermometers, stopwatches, and perfect air temperature are pretty silly as long as you have time to make the dough and allow for rising time. Making and eating homemade bread is one of the most pleasing and soothing activities available to the home or professional cook, and I hope you enjoy these.

Bread Tips

There are a few simple guidelines to follow when making bread. I strongly urge you to read up on bread baking in a basic bread book, which this is not.

Yeast: Yeast is a living fungus that, in the presence of flour, sugar, and water, grows and reproduces to make new cells. Carbon dioxide becomes trapped in the fibers of the dough, causing it to rise and expand. Most of the recipes in this chapter call for active dry yeast, which requires no special handling. Refrigerated, it keeps for months. To proof yeast, dissolve the amount called for in a recipe in a quarter cup of lukewarm water or milk (100°–110° F). If the yeast bubbles within 5 or 10 minutes, it is alive and usable. Temperatures over 120° F kill yeast. Too much salt, sugar, and fat inhibit the growth of yeast and therefore should not be added until the yeast has come to full potency. Two packages of active dry yeast = 1½ tablespoons compressed yeast.

Rising: Properly risen dough usually doubles in size. To check, make an indentation with two fingertips in the top of the dough. If the dough springs back it has not risen enough. When it no longer springs back, the rising process is complete.

Knead: Knead bread dough with both hands, folding and pushing the dough over on itself (see Fig. 1, page 17). The dough should be elastic and smooth. Ten to 20 minutes is usually enough time for hand kneading most doughs.

COOK'S NOTE

When blending ingredients for quick breads (breads without yeast), do not overmix. Overmixing makes dry, tough breads. Stir only long enough to combine the wet and dry ingredients.

Punch down: After the dough has risen once, it is sometimes necessary to punch it down, to stop the rising process instantly. Simply punch the dough with a fist until all the air has been released (see Fig. 2, below).

Sponge: A sponge is a loose batter consisting of yeast, liquid, and about a third the total amount of flour used in the recipe.

Wash: There are many washes for bread, each of which produces a different result. Many of the recipes in this book call for a wash to be applied before baking. An egg wash gives the bread a glossy sheen.

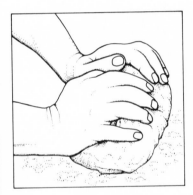 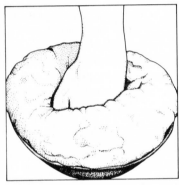

Fig. 1 Fold and push the dough over on itself.

Fig. 2 Punch the dough with your fist until all the air is released.

Fougasse

This flat yeast bread is usually made in a square or rectangular shape. Dimples are made on the surface of the bread and any assortment of toppings can be smoothed onto the top. This recipe makes two pieces of bread. One piece sliced in half through the center is enough for six sandwiches. You can make one with rosemary and one with onion or choose another topping for one of the halves to be eaten with another meal or for another sandwich. My brother Herb makes every kind of fougasse you can think of. When I asked him for a rosemary and an onion, he came up with this winning recipe.

Fougasse is versatile and can support many different toppings. Try olives, herbs, sun-dried tomatoes, or finely chopped nuts. It takes only a short time to bake.

Recommended Sandwiches for Fougasse
**Roast Beef and Rémoulade Cabbage
on Onion Fougasse** *(page 39)*
**Roast Lamb with Fried Garlic
on Rosemary Fougasse** *(page 53)*
**Tomato with Five-Olive Paste
on Rosemary Fougasse** *(page 80)*

Rosemary or Onion Fougasse

Mix the flours and yeast in a large bowl. Combine the salt, olive oil, and water. Add to the dry ingredients and mix until a soft dough forms. Make a ball and coat with the olive oil. Put the dough in a bowl and cover with plastic wrap or a damp towel and let rise in a warm, draft-free place for 2 hours or until doubled.

Punch the dough down, separate into two balls, and add the onions and rosemary to either or both. Knead into the dough and form each piece of dough into a flat disc, about 10 to 12 inches in diameter. Place uncovered on a greased cookie sheet in a warm spot and let rise until doubled, about 30 to 40 minutes. Make dimples on the surface of the dough with your fingertips. Brush with a little olive oil and sprinkle with coarse salt.

Preheat oven to 450° F.

Bake in the top third of the oven for 10 to 15 minutes or until golden brown.

Slice into wedges or rectangles for sandwiches.

Makes 2 loaves, enough for 12 sandwiches.

1 cup rye flour
3 cups all-purpose flour
½ cup semolina flour
5 tsp. active dry yeast
4 tsp. salt
¼ cup fruity olive oil
1¼ cups water
   (110°–115° F)
3 Tb. olive oil
2 Tb. chopped fresh
   rosemary
1 small onion, small diced
Coarse salt

Basic Egg Bread and Spice Bread Variation

This recipe for tender egg bread is from my friend Glen Mashy. While I was testing recipes for this book, he baked his bread in my kitchen so that we could sample sandwiches on the freshest bread. It also makes excellent toast; try my spiced variation for French Toast.

Egg bread provides a fairly neutral backdrop for other flavors. The spice variation, however, perks up a lazy sandwich, with its splash of spice in each bite. This bread also takes well to griddle cooking.

Recommended Sandwiches for Egg or Spice Bread
**Grilled Chicken, Mushroom, and Cheese
    on Egg Bread** *(page 88)*
**Grilled Three-Jewel Cheese Spread with Chicken
    on Spice Bread** *(page 92)*
Croque Monsieur on Spice Bread *(page 94)*

Scald the milk. Add the sugar and mix well. Cool the mixture to about 105° F and sprinkle the yeast on the surface. Stir well to incorporate and let sit for about 10 minutes.

Place the flour and salt in a large bowl. Stir the milk-yeast mixture, eggs, and oil into the flour. Mix well until the dough forms a ball. Turn out onto a floured surface and knead for 10 minutes, until smooth and elastic. Put the dough in a greased bowl, cover with a damp towel or plastic wrap, set in a warm, draft-free place, and let rise until double in size, about 1 hour.

Punch the dough down. To make the Spice Bread variation, grind all the spices to a coarse mixture and add them at this point. Divide the dough in half and knead each half for several minutes. Let rest for about 10 minutes. Divide each half into 3 long ropelike pieces. Make a braid and tuck the ends under. Place on a greased baking sheet, cover, and let rise in a warm place until doubled in size.

Brush with egg wash and sprinkle with poppy seeds.

Preheat oven to 400° F.

Bake for 15 minutes. Reduce the temperature to 375° F and bake for an additional 45 minutes.

Makes 2 loaves, enough for 12 to 16 sandwiches.

2¼ cups whole milk
3 Tb. plus 1 tsp. brown sugar
2 packages active dry yeast
6 cups all-purpose flour
1 Tb. salt
3 large eggs, lightly beaten
¼ cup vegetable oil
1 large egg, lightly beaten, for wash
2 Tb. poppy seeds, for garnish

SPICE BREAD VARIATION

2 tsp. fenugreek
2 tsp. anise seed
2 tsp. five-pepper mix
1 tsp. fennel seed
1 tsp. cloves
5 allspice
5 cardamom pods

Standard Bread

*T*his basic bread dough makes a tender and tasty loaf. Its combination of white and whole wheat flour ensures a perfect bread for sandwiches—not dense and not soft. The bread is not too assertive, which makes it a natural for additional flavoring agents such as olives, peppers, and chili spices.

Recommended Sandwiches for Standard Bread and Variations
**Smoked Duck with Apple-Pear Chutney
   on Chili Bread** *(page 43)*
Curried Scallop Salad on Pepper Bread *(page 47)*
Pepper-Nut Egg Salad on Olive Bread *(page 49)*
**Scrambled Eggs with Chinese Sausage and Peppers
   on Chili Bread Cheese Toast** *(page 68)*

3 cups milk
¼ cup brown sugar
1 cup powdered
   buttermilk
   (see COOK'S NOTE)
2 packages or 1½ Tb.
   active dry yeast
3½ cups all-purpose flour
3½ cups whole wheat
   flour
⅓ cup melted butter
4 tsp. salt
1 egg, lightly beaten,
   for wash

Scald the milk in a small saucepan. Dissolve the sugar and powdered buttermilk in the milk and cool to 90°–105° F, about 10 to 15 minutes.

Sprinkle the yeast on the surface of the milk mixture and stir lightly. Let sit for 10 minutes. (Yeast should foam within this time.)

Stir in 2 cups of the white flour and 2 cups of the whole wheat and beat vigorously for 5 minutes. Cover and let rise in a warm place until doubled in size, about 1 hour.

Fold in the melted butter, the salt, and the remaining flour. Mix until the dough pulls away from the sides of the bowl. Turn the dough out onto a floured surface and knead about 10 minutes or until elastic.

COOK'S NOTE:
You can find powdered buttermilk in most natural food stores and many grocery stores.

Put the dough in a greased bowl, cover, and let rise in a warm place until doubled in size, about 1 hour. Punch down and let rise for 40 to 50 minutes.

Divide the dough into two equal pieces. Shape into loaves and place in two greased 9-by-5-inch loaf pans. Let rise in a warm place for 20 to 25 minutes. Brush with egg wash.

Preheat oven to 350° F.

Bake for 1 hour or until the bread sounds hollow when tapped with fingertips.

Makes 2 loaves.

STANDARD BREAD VARIATIONS

After all the flour is incorporated into the dough, knead in the extra ingredients.

Olive Bread: Add 1½ cups chopped and pitted green olives.

Pepper Bread: Add 2 Tb. crushed black peppercorns, 2 Tb. crushed red peppercorns, and 3 Tb. finely minced fresh red pepper.

Chili Bread: Add 2 Tb. each ground cumin, coriander, oregano, and garlic powder and 1 Tb. cayenne or ground red chilies.

Black Bread

A rich and flavorful bread developed by my brother Herb. This recipe includes many special ingredients that add up to a healthful and tasty loaf of dark bread. The bread will improve in flavor for several days—if there is any left!

Black bread is usually very dense, but this version is tender and quite light in texture. The bread is perfect for all smoked meats, strong cheeses, and mustards. Dark bread is traditionally served with a hearty ale or stout. The flavors are robust and assertive, so take that into consideration when choosing sandwich ingredients.

Recommended Sandwiches for Black Bread
**Sardines, Onion, and Mustard Greens
 on Toasted Black Bread** *(page 67)*
**Baked Ham, Tilsit, and Dill Pickle
 on Black Bread** *(page 74)*
Reuben Sandwich *(page 89)*

1½ cups dark rye flour
2 cups all-purpose flour
2 Tb. unsweetened cocoa
1 Tb. freshly ground
 dark roasted coffee
 beans
1 Tb. caraway seed
2 Tb. brown sugar
2 Tb. active dry yeast
1 bottle Guinness stout
 (1½ cups)
Warm water
2 Tb. black molasses
1 Tb. salt
½ cup water
All-purpose flour, for
 kneading

Mix the rye flour, 1 cup of unbleached flour, cocoa, coffee, caraway seed, sugar, and yeast in a large bowl. Stir in the stout and enough warm water to make a dough the consistency of a thick cake batter. Stir vigorously for 5 minutes. Cover and let rise in a warm place until doubled in size, about 1½ to 2 hours.

Stir the batter down. Combine the molasses, salt, and water and add to the batter; mix well. Add the remaining cup of unbleached flour and stir well. When the dough is too dense to stir, transfer it to a floured surface and add additional white flour to form a dough just stiff enough to hold its shape. Knead 5 minutes. Cover and let rise in a warm place until doubled in size, about 1 hour.

Punch the dough down and shape into a flattened round. Place on a greased cookie sheet. Let rise about 20 minutes in a warm place or until size increases by one-third.

Preheat oven to 400° F.

Sprinkle the dough with a little white flour and spray with water. Place in top half of oven, spray oven with water, and bake for 10 minutes. Reduce the temperature to 350° F, place the bread on lower shelf, and spray oven with water. Bake for 35 to 40 minutes or until the bread sounds hollow when the bottom is tapped with fingertips.

Makes 1 large round or two small loaves.

Light Orange-Carrot Rye

I *must admit that this is my favorite bread. The carrot and orange are perfect accents for this slightly chewy light rye bread. It makes great toast and is terrific eating spread with sweet butter. Use this version of rye with subtle and refined sandwich ingredients to allow the flavor of the bread to come through.*

Recommended Sandwiches for Light Orange-Carrot Rye
**Smoked Ham with Yam Spread and Currants
    on Light Orange-Carrot Rye** *(page 77)*
Reuben Sandwich *(page 89)*

Combine the sponge ingredients in a bowl; mix well. Let rise in a warm place until bubbly, about 15 minutes.

Cook the carrot in ⅔ cup of water over low heat until tender. Drain, reserving the cooking water. Mash the carrot with a fork and set aside.

Combine the flours, salt, sugar, caraway seed, and zest; mix well. Add the sponge, carrot, and orange juice; mix. Add enough of the carrot cooking water to form a medium firm dough. Stir until the dough becomes too stiff to continue. Turn out onto a floured board and knead for 5 minutes. Place in a greased bowl, cover and let rise until doubled in size, about 1½ hours.

Punch the dough down, shape into an oval, fold in thirds lengthwise, and stretch to form a long loaf shape. Make a loaf about 3 inches wide and 20 inches long. Sprinkle a cookie sheet with cornmeal. Place the loaf seam side down on the cookie sheet. Using a sharp knife, make four or five 4-inch diagonal slashes on the surface of the bread. Let rise in a warm place until size has increased by one-third, 20 minutes to 1 hour.

Preheat oven to 400° F. Brush the loaf with egg wash. Bake in center of oven for 10 minutes. Spray oven with water. Rotate the bread, spray oven with water, and continue to bake for 25 to 30 minutes or until the bread sounds hollow when the bottom is tapped with fingertips.

Makes 1 large loaf, enough for 8 to 10 sandwiches.

SPONGE
1 Tb. active dry yeast
1 Tb. all-purpose flour
1 Tb. sugar
¼ cup water

1 medium carrot, cut into
    small pieces
⅔ cup water
2½ cups all-purpose flour
1 cup rye flour
2 tsp. sea salt
2 Tb. brown sugar
1 scant tsp. caraway seed
Zest and juice of 1 orange
2–3 Tb. cornmeal
1 large egg, lightly
    beaten, for wash

Onion-Rye Bagels

As far as I'm concerned, there aren't any bagels worth eating outside of New York. However, these are pretty tasty. Herb created a slightly chewy bagel with a fairly soft outer crust, which works well for sandwiches. These bagels are sublime with gravlax and caper cream cheese. The soft texture lends itself well to other sandwich ingredients.

Recommended Sandwich for Onion-Rye Bagels
**Onion-Rye Bagels with Gravlax
    and Caper Cream Cheese** *(page 114)*

SPONGE
1 Tb. active dry yeast
1 Tb. all-purpose flour
1 tsp. brown sugar
¼ cup water

1½ cups rye flour
2 cups all-purpose flour
2 Tb. brown sugar
¾ cup water
2 tsp. salt
1 cup minced onion
½ Tb. butter
Cornmeal, for baking

GLAZE
1 egg yolk
½ tsp. sugar
¼ tsp. salt
½ tsp. water

Combine the sponge ingredients; mix well. Let rise in a warm place until bubbly, about 15 minutes.

Combine 1 cup rye flour, 1 cup all-purpose flour, and the sugar. Add the sponge and water to this mixture. Stir vigorously for 5 minutes. Cover and let rise in a warm place until doubled in size, about 1½ hours. Stir down.

Combine the salt, remaining flours, and half the onion. Add to the dough. Stir until the dough is stiff. Turn out onto a floured surface and knead for 5 minutes, adding additional all-purpose flour to make a smooth, elastic dough. Form a ball and roll in a bowl greased with the butter. Cover and let rise in a warm place until doubled in size, about 1½ hours.

Punch the dough down and divide into 10 equal balls.

Press a hole in each ball, making bagel shapes (see illustration below). Place the formed dough on a cookie sheet and let rise about 20 minutes.

Bring 3 to 4 quarts of water to a boil in a shallow pan.

Preheat oven to 400° F.

Drop the bagels into the boiling water and cook about 3 to 4 minutes on each side. Remove and let drain on a towel.

Sprinkle about 2 tablespoons cornmeal on a cookie sheet.

Arrange the bagels on the cookie sheet. Combine the glaze ingredients and brush the bagels with the glaze. Sprinkle the remaining minced onion on the top of the bagels. Bake in the top third of the oven for 30 to 35 minutes or until browned. Cool on a wire rack.

Makes 10 bagels.

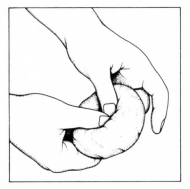

Press a hole in each ball of dough to make a bagel shape.

Pesto-Pistachio Bread

This rich and sumptuous bread is irresistible for good reason. Garlicky pesto made with nutty Asiago cheese forms a bright green pattern through the bread. Pistachio nuts are the perfect accent. Pesto-Pistachio Bread is delicious any time of day or night with or without butter. The oil and cheese from the pesto make this bread so moist and flavorful that you don't need additional butter or cheese to spark the taste. "Gilding the lily" is, however, one of my specialties. Combine this bread with some tempting sandwich ingredients for an unforgettable meal.

Recommended Sandwiches for Pesto-Pistachio Bread
**Herbed Seafood and Summer Vegetable Salad
      on Pesto-Pistachio Bread** (*page 40*)
**Italian Goat Cheese Spread
      on Pesto-Pistachio Bread** (*page 42*)

3 cups fresh basil
4 cloves garlic
1 tsp. salt
½ tsp. black pepper
1½ cups grated Asiago
   cheese
½ cup olive oil
2 packages active dry
   yeast
2 Tb. sugar
1 cup warm water
   (about 110°–115° F)
1 cup warm milk
   (about 110°–115° F)
5 cups all-purpose flour
1 cup whole wheat flour
2 tsp. salt
1 cup pistachios, coarsely
   chopped
2 Tb. cornmeal
1 large egg, lightly
   beaten, for wash

Place the basil, garlic, salt, pepper, cheese, and olive oil in a blender and purée until fairly smooth. Set aside.

Dissolve the yeast and sugar in the water and milk; mix well. Add the flours, salt, and pistachios and mix to form a dough. Turn out onto a floured surface and knead the dough for 10 minutes until smooth and elastic. Cover and let rise until doubled in size, about 1½ hours.

Preheat oven to 350° F.

Punch down the dough and knead for 3 minutes. Cover and let the dough rest for 10 minutes. Roll it out to a 12-by-17-inch

Fig. 1 Spread the pesto on the surface of the dough, leaving a one-inch border.

Fig. 2 Roll the dough up, jelly-roll fashion, keeping the pesto on the inside.

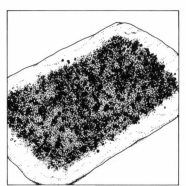

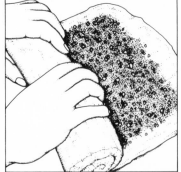

rectangle. Spread the pesto on the surface of the dough, leaving a 1-inch border (see Fig. 1, page 28). Roll up the dough, jelly-roll fashion, keeping the pesto on the inside (see Fig. 2, page 28). Let rise for 10 minutes. Sprinkle a cookie sheet with corn-meal. Brush the dough with the egg and place on cookie sheet. Bake in oven 45 to 50 minutes, until the bread sounds hollow when the bottom is tapped with fingertips. Cool on a wire rack.

Makes 1 large loaf, enough for 10 or 12 sandwiches.

Corn Bread

*T*his is my style of bread making—no yeast, no rising, and no punching. *In less than 45 minutes you can produce a moist and firm corn bread that goes with the more elaborate flavors of a sandwich. Do not overmix the dry and wet ingredients or the bread will be tough.*

Recommended Sandwiches for Corn Bread
**Barbecued Pork with Marinated Green Beans
    on Corn Bread** *(page 102)*
**Two-Pepper Chicken Salad with Pumpkin Seeds and
    Chipotle Mayonnaise on Corn Bread** *(page 109)*

Preheat oven to 425° F.

Combine the dry ingredients in a bowl; mix well. Combine the milk, egg, butter, and chicken fat in a small bowl. Add the wet ingredients to the dry and mix just enough to combine. Pour the batter into a well-greased 9-inch-square pan. Bake for 20 to 25 minutes or until a toothpick comes out clean when inserted into center of the bread. Cool and store in a plastic bag.

Makes 1 round corn bread, enough for 6 sandwiches.

¾ cup all-purpose flour
1¼ cups yellow stone-
    ground cornmeal
1 tsp. baking powder
1 Tb. white sugar
1 Tb. brown sugar
1 tsp. salt
1 cup milk
1 large egg, lightly beaten
2 Tb. unsalted butter,
    melted
1 Tb. chicken fat, melted
    (optional)

Date-Nut Bread

*M*y *mom used to make this moist and nutty bread around the holidays, but I would beg her to make it all the time. Plump sweet dates and crisp walnuts make for a satisfying and pleasing sandwich bread. You can think of many delicious combinations for sandwiches with this traditional quick bread.*

Recommended Sandwiches for Date-Nut Bread
Sweet English on Date-Nut Bread *(page 38)*
Peanut Butter-Banana on Date-Nut Bread *(page 51)*
**Ham, Bitter Greens, and Melted Brie
on Date-Nut Bread** *(page 72)*

2½ cups all-purpose flour
3 Tb. brown sugar
2 tsp. baking powder
1½ tsp. salt
1 tsp. cinnamon
¾ cup chopped walnuts
2 eggs, lightly beaten
1 cup milk
3 Tb. unsalted butter,
  melted
⅔ cup chopped dates
  (see COOK'S NOTE)

Preheat oven to 350° F.

Combine the dry ingredients in a large bowl; mix well. Combine the eggs, milk, and butter in a small bowl; mix well. Add the wet ingredients to the dry and mix just enough to combine the ingredients. Add the dates and stir to incorporate. Pour the batter into a greased 9-by-5-inch loaf pan. Bake for 50 to 60 minutes or until a toothpick comes out clean when inserted into the center of the bread.

Makes 1 loaf, enough for 6 to 8 sandwiches.

COOK'S NOTE:

Freeze the dates for at least 1 hour to make chopping easier.

Maple-Pecan Bread

I *often persuade my mother to make this bread for me. In the days of old, bourbon was considered a strange ingredient for bread. But the bourbon and maple make a perfect taste combination, along with the pecans. If you can resist eating this bread plain, you will find that it makes some pretty special sandwiches. The combination of sweet and nutty with savory is an exciting sensation for the palate.*

Recommended Sandwiches for Maple-Pecan Bread
Citrus Spread and Fruit on Maple-Pecan Bread *(page 46)*
Bacon and Teleme Melt on Maple-Pecan Bread *(page 72)*
**Apricot Cream Cheese and Pears
    on Maple-Pecan Bread** *(page 111)*

Preheat oven to 350° F.

Cream the butter and sugar together until light and fluffy. Add the eggs, syrup, vanilla, buttermilk, and bourbon; mix well.

Combine the flour, baking powder, baking soda, salt, and mace in a large bowl; mix well. Add the wet ingredients to the dry, stirring to prevent lumps. Add the pecans; mix just enough to incorporate the ingredients.

Pour the batter into a greased 9-by-5-inch loaf pan. Bake for 55 minutes to 1 hour, or until a toothpick comes out clean when inserted into the center of the bread.

Makes 1 loaf, enough for 6 to 8 sandwiches.

½ cup butter, softened
⅓ cup brown sugar
2 eggs
⅔ cup maple syrup
1 Tb. vanilla extract
½ cup buttermilk
3 Tb. bourbon
2 cups all-purpose flour
1 tsp. baking powder
½ tsp. baking soda
1 tsp. salt
½ tsp. mace
1 cup chopped pecans

Pumpkin-Spice Bread

2 cups all-purpose flour
2 tsp. baking powder
½ tsp. baking soda
½ tsp. cinnamon
½ tsp. nutmeg
½ tsp. ground cardamom
½ tsp. black pepper
1 tsp. salt
½ cup chopped walnuts
1 cup cooked pumpkin
(see COOK'S NOTE)
⅔ cup sugar
½ cup milk
1 tsp. vanilla extract
2 eggs, lightly beaten
3 Tb. unsalted butter,
melted

COOK'S NOTE:

I usually shy away from canned goods. However, because canned pumpkin has a consistent flavor and texture, I recommend it for this bread.

*M*y mom gave me this recipe for tender, spicy, moist bread when I told her about one of the wacky sandwiches I had planned for the book. It goes very well with salty or spicy hot sandwich ingredients. Avoid putting soggy or wet ingredients on this bread.

Recommended Sandwiches for Pumpkin-Spice Bread
Smoked Ham and Pickled Onions with Apple-Carrot Purée on Pumpkin-Spice Bread *(page 45)*
Roast Pepper and Hot Coppa on Pumpkin-Spice Bread *(page 54)*

Preheat oven to 350° F.
Combine the dry ingredients in a large bowl; mix well. Combine the pumpkin, sugar, milk, vanilla, eggs, and butter in another bowl; mix well. Add the wet ingredients to the dry, stirring just enough to mix. Pour the batter into a greased 9-by-5-inch loaf pan. Bake for 1 hour or until a toothpick comes out clean when inserted into the center of the bread.
Makes 1 loaf, enough for 6 to 8 sandwiches.

Cornmeal Brioche

*M*y generous friend Beth Hensperger offered me this recipe when I complained about having trouble making brioche. She is a master baker, but assured me that this recipe would be easy and quite delicious. I bake the bread in a loaf pan for easier sandwich making. You may also bake the dough in the traditional brioche molds.

Recommended Sandwiches for Cornmeal Brioche
Prosciutto, Figs, and Orange with Port Butter on Toasted Brioche *(page 76)*
Grilled Eggplant and Mozzarella with Roast Peppers on Sun-Dried Tomato Brioche *(page 86)*

Combine ½ cup of the flour, the cornmeal, yeast, sugar, and salt; mix well. Add the hot water and beat vigorously by hand for 5 minutes. Add the eggs one at a time, beating well after each addition. Gradually add 1½ cups flour; mix well. Add the butter a few pieces at a time; beat just until incorporated. Gradually add 1½ cups flour and beat until well incorporated and creamy. The dough will be very soft and batter-like.

Pour the batter into a greased bowl, cover tightly, and let rise at room temperature (see COOK'S NOTE) until doubled in size, about 2 to 3 hours.

Gently deflate the dough with a spoon, cover tightly, and refrigerate 12 hours or overnight for easier handling.

Turn the chilled dough out onto a lightly floured surface. Divide in half and form into loaves. Place in two 8-by-4-inch greased loaf pans; the dough should not fill more than half of each pan. Let rise at room temperature (see COOK'S NOTE) until doubled in size, about 1½ hours or until the dough is level with the top of the pans.

Preheat oven to 375° F.

Bake for 40 to 45 minutes or until a toothpick comes out clean when inserted into the center of the bread. Remove from pans to cool completely.

Makes 2 loaves.

SUN-DRIED TOMATO VARIATION

After incorporating the eggs, add ½ cup chopped oil-packed sun-dried tomatoes, fully drained.

3½ cups all-purpose flour
1 cup yellow cornmeal
1 package active dry yeast
2 Tb. sugar
2 tsp. salt
½ cup hot water
  (110°–115° F)
5 eggs, room temperature
½ pound unsalted butter,
  cut into ½-inch pieces

COOK'S NOTE:
The butter will separate from the dough if left to rise in a warm area.

California Walnut Bread

*A*nother marvelous bread from baking genius Beth. The combination of meaty walnuts and walnut oil in a yeast bread is a true delight. The bread is firm and flavorful, perfect for sandwiches.

Recommended Sandwiches for California Walnut Bread
**Grilled Flank Steak with Cucumber and Radish
on Walnut Bread with Orange Butter** *(page 44)*
**Grilled Duck with Apple-Apricot Chutney
on California Walnut Bread** *(page 59)*

SPONGE
**2 packages active dry
 yeast**
**¼ cup warm water
 (105°–115° F)**
2 cups all-purpose flour
3 Tb. sugar
**2 cups milk, room
 temperature**

½ cup walnut oil
1 Tb. salt
**1¼ cups lightly toasted
 chopped walnuts**
**About 3 cups all-purpose
 flour**
**1 egg, lightly beaten,
 for wash**

Sprinkle the yeast over the warm water and stir to dissolve. Let stand until bubbly, about 10 minutes.

Meanwhile, combine the flour, sugar, and milk in a large bowl. Whisk vigorously and add the yeast mixture. Cover with plastic wrap and let rest ½ hour in a warm place until bubbly.

Add the oil, salt, and walnuts to the sponge. Add ½ cup of flour at a time until a stiff dough is formed. Turn out onto a floured surface and gently knead until smooth, soft, and elastic. The dough will be moist and soft. Too much flour makes a dry bread, so add the flour with care. Cover with plastic wrap and let rise in a warm place until doubled in size, about 1 hour.

Turn the dough out and divide in half. Form into 2 round loaves. Place on a greased sheet pan lined with parchment paper. Cover loosely and let rise again in a warm area, about 40 minutes.

Brush with egg wash. Bake for 35 to 40 minutes or until the bread sounds hollow when the bottom is tapped with fingertips. Cool on a wire rack.

Makes 2 large round loaves.

Corn Tortillas

Most major supermarkets sell corn and flour tortillas. Close to my neighborhood, in the Mission District of San Francisco, I can watch Latin-American women with pleasing faces and strong hands pat the dough to make sturdy fresh corn tortillas, thicker than those made by machine. You can make your own corn tortillas with Masa Harina or corn flour, not cornmeal. I'm sure you will be delighted with these peasant-style tortillas.

Recommended Sandwiches for Corn Tortillas
**Grilled Flank Steak, Pinto Bean Spread,
 and Feta Cheese with Corn Tortillas** *(page 60)*
**Roast Pork with Avocado-Jicama Salsa
 on Corn Tortillas** *(page 113)*

Combine the flour and salt. Mix in the water with a fork. Stir until a fairly soft dough forms. Turn out onto a dry surface and knead for 3 to 5 minutes. Let rest for 5 minutes. Working with 2 or 3 tablespoons of dough at a time, roll into balls and flatten with your hands. Pat the balls into flat ½- to ¼-inch thick discs, varying the size if desired.

Heat a thin layer of vegetable oil in a large skillet. Cook the tortillas over moderate heat until golden brown on one side, then flip and cook until golden brown on the other side. Keep warm in a low oven until ready to use or cool and store in a plastic bag. The dough and the cooked tortillas keep for only a day or two. The taste is quite different from the store-bought machine-made variety.

Makes about 12 to 15 tortillas, depending on the size.

2 cups Masa Harina (corn
 flour)
1 tsp. salt
1¼ to 1½ cups water
Vegetable oil, for cooking

Navajo Fry Bread

This simple-to-make savory treat is a delicious snack all on its own. It makes a tasty accompaniment to soups and salads as well as an unusual holder for sandwich fillings and toppings.

Recommended Sandwiches for Navajo Fry Bread
**Roast Pork, Smoked Cheese, and Tomato Salsa
on Navajo Fry Bread** *(page 103)*
**Five-Spice Chicken, Daikon, and Curry Mayonnaise
on Navajo Fry Bread** *(page 104)*
**Grilled Flank Steak, Gorgonzola, and Greens
on Navajo Fry Bread** *(page 105)*

1⅔ cups all-purpose flour
⅓ cup Masa Harina
½ cup instant nonfat
  dry milk
2 tsp. baking powder
1 tsp. each, ground
  coriander and
  cumin seed
½ tsp. salt
2 Tb. vegetable
  shortening
¾ to 1 cup water
1½ to 2 cups vegetable
  oil, for cooking

Combine the flour, Masa Harina, nonfat milk, baking powder, spices, and salt in a large bowl; mix well. Add the shortening and rub the mixture with cool fingers until it resembles coarse meal. Add the water a little at a time, mixing with a fork, until the mixture clings together. Form the dough into a ball and knead on a floured surface for 2 or 3 minutes. Divide the dough into 6 equal balls; cover with plastic wrap and set aside. Dough may be made up to 8 hours ahead and stored, wrapped in plastic, in the refrigerator.

Flatten each ball into a 6-inch disc. Heat about 2 inches of oil in a large skillet. When the oil is hot, but not smoking, add the dough and fry until puffy and golden brown. Do not crowd the dough because it will not cook properly. Remove the bread from skillet and drain on paper towels. Keep warm in a low oven until all the dough has been fried.

Makes 6 to 8 servings.

Sandwich Recipes

Room-Temperature Sandwiches

In olden times this chapter would have been called Cold Sandwiches or Chilled Sandwiches. Most cold food is difficult to taste, but at room temperature the natural flavors are released and seem more intense. The following sandwiches are designed to be served at room temperature.

Sweet English on Date-Nut Bread

This unusual combination makes a light brunch or snack any time of day. You can combine the ingredients and assemble the sandwich in minutes. Smooth and slightly sweet banana is a good complement to the flavorful Stilton cheese.

BANANA SPREAD
1 plaintain or 2 firm but ripe bananas
Pinch each, salt, white pepper, nutmeg, and mace

12 slices Date-Nut Bread (see page 30)
1 bunch rocket, leaves only
½–⅔ pound English Stilton cheese, crumbled

Mash the plaintain or bananas with a fork, add the spices, and mix well. Taste and adjust seasoning.

Spread a fairly thin layer of the banana spread on each slice of bread; top with rocket. Crumble the Stilton cheese over the rocket. Cover with a second piece of bread.

Makes 4 to 6 servings.

Roast Beef and Rémoulade Cabbage on Onion Fougasse

*T*he cabbage portion of this sandwich is delicious on its own, and it makes a wonderful juicy accompaniment to the meat and bread.

Remove the meat from the refrigerator at least 2 hours before cooking.

Preheat oven to 500° F.

Rub the garlic over the meat, sprinkle with salt and pepper. Place the meat fat side up on a rack in a shallow greased roasting pan. Insert a meat thermometer in the thickest part of the meat, away from bone or fat. Cook for about 45 minutes or until the thermometer reads 120° F. Remove the meat from the oven and allow to cool to room temperature before slicing.

Combine the sauce ingredients in a large bowl. Add the cabbage, onion, and garlic. Mix well; taste and adjust the seasoning.

Place some of the cabbage mixture on the squares of bread. Top with thinly sliced roast beef, more cabbage, and more bread.

Makes 6 to 8 servings.

2 to 2½ pounds rolled eye of round (see COOK'S NOTE)
5 cloves garlic, minced
Salt and pepper

RÉMOULADE SAUCE
1 cup Mayonnaise (see page 12)
2 Tb. chopped dill pickle
2 Tb. capers
1 Tb. Dijon mustard
3 Tb. minced fresh parsley
2 tsp. each, minced fresh tarragon, chervil, and thyme
3 tsp. anchovy paste
1 Tb. sherry vinegar

1 small head white cabbage, shredded
1 small red onion, sliced thin
2 cloves garlic, minced

Onion Fougasse (see page 19)

COOK'S NOTE:
Leftover roast beef can be used for cold salads or any number of sandwiches.

Herbed Seafood and Summer Vegetable Salad on Pesto-Pistachio Bread

This colorful seafood salad combines the delicate flavors of summer produce. The bread is the perfect companion.

½ pound small prawns, unpeeled

½ pound bay scallops

1 Tb. unsalted butter

½ pound bay shrimp

10 spears asparagus, trimmed, and diced small

1 small red pepper, diced small

1 small ear corn, shaved

¾ cup Mayonnaise (see page 12)

3 Tb. minced mixed fresh herbs (parsley, thyme, chives, dill)

2 green onions, minced

Salt and pepper, to taste

Lettuce

Butter

12 slices Pesto-Pistachio Bread (see page 28)

6 slices tomato, for garnish (optional)

Cook the prawns in boiling water for 1 to 2 minutes, depending on their size. Drain and cool. Remove the shells and tails and chop the meat into ½-inch pieces. Remove the small muscle from the sides of each scallop. In a large sauté pan, cook the scallops in the butter for 1 minute, stirring often. Drain and cool. Combine the prawns, scallops, and bay shrimp in a large bowl.

Blanch the asparagus in salted boiling water for 1 minute; refresh in iced water, drain, and cool. Add the asparagus, red pepper, and corn to the seafood; mix well.

Combine the mayonnaise, herbs, and green onions in a large bowl; mix well. Add the seafood and vegetables. Season with salt and pepper.

Place pieces of lettuce on 6 slices of buttered bread and top with salad and tomato. Cover with more lettuce and a second slice of bread.

Makes 6 to 8 servings.

Roast Pork with Beet Relish on Pumpernickel

Tangy red beets are the perfect complement to thinly sliced roast pork. You may make the beet relish a day ahead and cook the meat just before serving.

Soak the onions and currants in the rice wine vinegar for 1 hour.
Preheat oven to 500° F.
Rub the pork with olive oil and garlic. Press the black pepper into the meat. Place the loin fat side up on a rack in a greased roasting pan. Insert a meat thermometer into the center of the meat. Cook at 500° F for 3 minutes, reduce oven heat to 325° F, and roast about 20 to 25 minutes for each pound of pork. The thermometer should read 155° F. Remove the meat from oven and cool at room temperature. Slice as thinly as possible. Wrap and set aside until ready to use.
Cook the beets in simmering water for 30 to 40 minutes or until very tender when pierced with a fork. Drain and peel. In a food processor, purée the beets and apple juice until smooth. Drain the onions and currants and combine with the apple, orange zest, spices, and raspberry vinegar. Mix well, taste, and season with salt and pepper. Let sit at room temperature until ready to use.
Combine the horseradish and mayonnaise and spread some on 6 slices of the bread and layer the meat on it. Spoon beet relish over the meat and top each with a second slice of bread.
Makes 6 servings.

1 medium red onion, diced small
⅓ cup currants
½ cup seasoned rice wine vinegar
1 pork loin, rolled and tied
Olive oil
3 cloves garlic, minced
2 Tb. coarsely cracked black pepper
2 medium red beets, trimmed and washed
⅓ cup apple juice
1 small green apple, peeled and cored, diced small
Zest of 1 small orange
½ tsp. ground coriander
Pinch each, nutmeg, mace, cardamom
2 Tb. raspberry vinegar
Salt and pepper, to taste

3 Tb. freshly ground horseradish or ¼ cup prepared
¾ cup Mayonnaise (see page 12)
12 slices pumpernickel

Italian Goat Cheese Spread
on Pesto-Pistachio Bread

¾ pound natural cream
cheese (see COOK'S
NOTE)

⅓ pound goat cheese

1 large clove garlic,
minced

⅔ cup sun-dried
tomatoes, coarsely
chopped

½ cup walnuts, toasted
and coarsely chopped

⅔ cup chopped fresh
basil

3 Tb. each, minced fresh
chives, oregano, and
thyme

Pinch of red pepper
flakes

Salt and pepper, to taste

12 slices·tomato

1 bunch watercress, large
stems removed

12 slices Pesto-Pistachio
Bread (see page 28)

COOK'S NOTE:

Natural cream cheese con-
tains no added chemicals,
stabilizers, or gum. For a
stronger goat cheese flavor,
use more goat cheese and
less cream cheese. The intensity also depends on the
type, variety, and age of
the goat cheese.

*T*his simple spread, made crunchy with toasted walnuts, is a
delicious topping for any bread or cracker. Sun-dried tomatoes add a unique flavor.

In a large bowl, combine the cream cheese and goat cheese.
Whip by hand or with an electric mixer until soft and creamy.
Add the garlic, sun-dried tomatoes, walnuts, basil, herbs, and
red pepper flakes; mix well. Season with salt and pepper.

Spread some of the cheese mixture on each slice of bread.
Cover 6 of the slices with tomatoes and watercress. Top with a
second slice of cheese-covered bread. Serve immediately.

Makes 6 servings.

Smoked Duck with Apple-Pear Chutney on Chili Bread

*F*resh duck may be substituted for the smoked, but the combination of sweet and hot go very well with a smoky meat taste. The chutney improves the second day.

Cook the onion, garlic, jalapeño pepper, and spices in the butter in a large sauté pan over high heat for 2 to 3 minutes, stirring constantly. Add the sherry and cook over high heat for 1 minute; reduce the heat and cook over low heat until the onion is translucent. Add the apple, pear, raisins, ginger, and apple juice and cook over moderate heat until the fruit is tender, but not mushy. Season with salt and pepper. Cool the chutney, add the toasted pecans; taste and adjust the seasoning.

Spread 12 slices of bread with a thin layer of mayonnaise. Arrange lettuce leaves on 6 slices of bread. Spoon about 3 tablespoons of chutney over the lettuce. Place some duck on top of the chutney and cover with lettuce and a second slice of bread.

Makes 6 servings.

CHUTNEY

1 medium onion, diced small

1 clove garlic, minced

1 red jalapeño pepper, minced

½ tsp. each, ground coriander, cumin seed, anise seed

Pinch each, ground fenugreek, nutmeg, and cinnamon

3 Tb. unsalted butter

Splash dry sherry

1 large green apple, peeled and diced small

1 large pear, peeled and diced small

½ cup golden raisins

2 Tb. minced fresh ginger

⅓ cup apple juice

Salt and pepper, to taste

⅔ cup toasted pecans

12 slices Chili Bread (see page 23)

½ cup Mayonnaise (see page 12)

1 large head butter lettuce

1½ pounds smoked duck meat (see COOK'S NOTE)

COOK'S NOTE:

Buy a whole smoked duck and remove the meat from the bones, or use smoked duck breast.

Grilled Flank Steak with Cucumber and Radish on Walnut Bread with Orange Butter

*T*his sandwich is popular simply because of the meat! If you can resist eating the steak before it gets between the bread, I guarantee a delicious and filling sandwich, complete with vegetables and crunch.

MARINADE
¾ cup olive oil
¼ cup red wine
¼ cup soy sauce
¼ cup honey
3 cloves garlic, minced
1 tsp. each, black pepper, oregano, and thyme

1½ pounds flank steak

3 Tb. unsalted butter, softened
⅓ pound natural cream cheese
Zest of 1 small orange
Pinch each, white pepper, nutmeg, and cayenne

12 slices California Walnut Bread (see page 34)
6 to 8 radishes, trimmed and sliced thin
1 small English cucumber, peeled and sliced thin

Combine the marinade ingredients and pour over the steak. Place the marinade and steak in a heavy plastic bag and seal tightly. Marinate overnight in the refrigerator or 3 hours at room temperature.

Prepare a charcoal grill.

While you wait for the coals to get hot, combine the butter, cream cheese, zest, and spices. Mix until creamy and smooth. Taste and adjust seasoning.

When the coals are red hot, place the steak on the grill. Cook approximately 5 to 7 minutes per side—the thicker the steak, the longer the cooking time. When the steak is done, remove it from the grill and let sit for 10 to 15 minutes. Slice the meat as thinly as possible.

Spread orange butter on 12 slices of bread. Arrange a thin layer of radishes, then cucumbers over the butter. Cover 6 of the bread slices with meat. Carefully top each with a second slice of bread.

Makes 6 servings.

Smoked Ham and Pickled Onions with Apple-Carrot Purée on Pumpkin-Spice Bread

The moist and flavorful pumpkin bread is perfect for these comforting and familiar autumn ingredients.

Cut the onion in half; peel and slice ¼ inch thick. Place in a large heat-resistant bowl.

Place the vinegar, water, bay leaves, and spices in a saucepan. Bring to a boil and pour over the onions. Let the onions sit at room temperature until cool. Cover and store in refrigerator.

Melt the butter in a sauté pan. Add the apples, carrots, and spices and cook over low heat, covered, until the fruit is tender. Purée in a food processor or blender. When the mixture is smooth, add the maple syrup. Season with salt and pepper.

Spread apple-carrot purée on 6 slices of the bread and top with ham and drained pickled onions. Spread mayonnaise on the remaining bread slices and place over the onions.

Makes 6 servings.

1 medium red onion
¼ cup apple cider vinegar
1 cup water
2 bay leaves
1 tsp. each, black peppercorns, fennel seed, and caraway seed
3 Tb. unsalted butter
2 medium green apples, peeled and coarsely chopped
2 medium carrots, peeled and diced small
Pinch each, coriander, nutmeg, mace, and cardamom
2 Tb. pure maple syrup
Salt and pepper, to taste

12 slices Pumpkin-Spice Bread (see page 32)
1–1½ pounds smoked ham, sliced thin
Mayonnaise (see page 12)

Citrus Spread and Fruit on Maple-Pecan Bread

*T*his toasty and nutty bread makes a wonderful backdrop for the lively and fresh tastes of the fruit and spread. A good brunch offering.

½ pound natural cream cheese, softened

3 Tb. unsalted butter, softened

Zest of 1 large orange

Zest of 1 each, lemon, lime, and tangerine

Juice of 1 each, orange, lemon, lime, and tangerine

Salt and white pepper, to taste

1 large red apple

1 large firm pear

12 slices Maple-Pecan Bread (see page 31)

½ pint raspberries

½ pint blueberries

Combine the cream cheese, butter, zest, and juices in a bowl. Mix well, taste, and season with salt and pepper.

Cut the apple and pear in half and remove the cores. With the cut side down, cut thin slices of the fruit.

Cover 12 slices of bread with the citrus spread. Alternate pieces of apple and pear on 6 of the bread slices, then sprinkle them with raspberries and blueberries. Cover with the remaining 6 slices of bread.

Makes 6 servings.

Curried Scallop Salad
on Pepper Bread

Tender scallops and Indian spices make this an unusual sandwich. Serve a mellow fruit salad and a spicy sauvignon blanc with it for a complete meal.

Melt the butter in a large sauté pan. Cook the onion, garlic, and spices over high heat for 2 minutes, stirring constantly. Add the wine, reduce the heat, and cook until the onion is soft and the wine has evaporated. Add the scallops and cook over moderate heat for 1 to 2 minutes, until the scallops are tender. Do not overcook the scallops. Drain the scallop mixture through a fine strainer. Cool and place in a large bowl.

Add the celery, green onions, cilantro, vinegar, and ½ cup mayonnaise to the scallops and onions, mix well; season with salt and pepper.

Spread a thin layer of mayonnaise on 12 slices of bread. Layer radishes on 6 of the slices, top with the scallop salad, and cover each with a second slice of bread.

Makes 6 servings.

3 Tb. unsalted butter

1 small onion, diced small

1 clove garlic, minced

½ tsp. each, ground cumin and coriander

¼ tsp. each, ground fenugreek, mace, anise seed, and turmeric

½ cup dry white wine

1 pound bay scallops, small muscle removed

2 small tender stalks celery, diced small

3 green onions, minced

¼ cup chopped cilantro

1 Tb. sherry vinegar

½ cup Mayonnaise, plus additional for bread (see page 12)

Salt and pepper, to taste

12 slices Pepper Bread (see page 23)

6 large radishes, trimmed and sliced paper thin

Pecan-Fig Cream Cheese on Bran Muffins

This fast and easy spread makes breakfast or brunch a pleasure. Prepare the tasty Pecan-Fig Cream Cheese the day before. The next morning bake your favorite bran muffins or, even easier, pick up some from your neighborhood bakery. The recipe works well with any favorite sweet muffin.

¼ cup coarsely chopped dry figs

½ cup orange liqueur

¾–1 pound natural cream cheese, softened

¾ cup toasted pecans, coarsely chopped

Pinch each, nutmeg, cinnamon, and black pepper

½ cup coarsely chopped fresh figs

6 bran muffins

Soak the dry figs in the orange liqueur for 1 to 2 hours. Drain and place the figs in a large bowl. Add the cream cheese, pecans, and spices; mix well. Add the fresh figs and stir gently to combine with the other ingredients.

Slice each muffin in half, crosswise, then crosswise in half again (see Fig. 1, below). Spread some of the cream cheese on each piece of muffin, except for the top piece. Fit the pieces together to form one muffin with 4 layers (see Fig. 2, below).

Makes 6 servings.

Fig. 1 Slice bran muffin in half crosswise, then slice each half crosswise again.

Fig. 2 Spread cream cheese filling on each muffin slice except the top, and assemble.

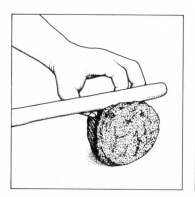

Pepper-Nut Egg Salad on Olive Bread

Roasted peanuts give this old standby a new twist. Olive Bread is an excellent taste companion for the colorful egg salad.

Soak the onion in the vinegar for at least 1 hour. Drain and discard the vinegar.

Place the remaining ingredients except the bread and lettuce in a bowl; mix well. Taste and adjust the seasoning.

Spread a little mayonnaise on 12 slices of bread, cover 6 of the slices with a lettuce leaf, top with the salad, and cover each with lettuce and a second slice of bread.

Makes 6 servings.

1 small onion, diced small
3 Tb. rice wine vinegar
12 hard-boiled eggs, coarsely chopped
1 medium red pepper, diced small
1 medium green pepper, diced small
1 small jalapeño pepper, minced
¾ cup roasted peanuts, coarsely chopped (see COOK'S NOTE)
2 tsp. ground coriander
Pinch each, ground celery seed and caraway seed
½ cup coarsely chopped cilantro
¾ cup Mayonnaise, plus additional for bread (see page 12)
Salt and pepper, to taste

12 slices Olive Bread (see page 23)
12 leaves green leaf lettuce

COOK'S NOTE:

The salad can be made up to 6 hours ahead, but don't add the peanuts or assemble the sandwiches until just before serving, to prevent the sandwiches from becoming soggy.

Grilled Lamb, Peppers, and Tahini Spread with Pita

Tender lamb, crisp peppers, and smooth and creamy tahini spread make this a Middle Eastern favorite. Prepare the tahini a day ahead so the flavors can develop.

MARINADE
¾ cup olive oil
3 cloves garlic, minced
Juice of 3 lemons
2 Tb. prepared mustard
3 sprigs rosemary
1 Tb. each, dry thyme, oregano, sage, and black pepper

3 lamb loins, about ¾ pound each
⅔ cup tahini
1 clove garlic, minced
Juice of 2 lemons
½ cup Mayonnaise (see page 12)
1 small red pepper, julienned
1 small green pepper, julienned
1 small onion, sliced thin
1 ear corn, shaved
½ cup pitted and chopped Calamata olives
¼ cup minced fresh parsley
¼ cup coarsely chopped fresh mint
2 Tb. red wine vinegar
Salt and pepper, to taste

6–8 pita breads, sliced in half

Combine the marinade ingredients. Marinate the lamb in the refrigerator overnight or for 3 hours at room temperature, turning often to distribute the marinade ingredients.

Combine the tahini, garlic, and lemon juice; mix well. Add the mayonnaise to make a smooth paste. Set aside.

Combine the peppers, onion, corn, olives, parsley, mint, and vinegar in a large bowl. Add salt and pepper.

Prepare a charcoal grill.

When the coals are red hot, place the meat on the grill and cook it about 3 minutes per side. The cooking time will depend on the thickness of the meat, the heat from the coals, and how you like your meat cooked. When the lamb is done, remove it from the grill and set aside for 10 to 15 minutes before slicing into thin strips.

Place the pitas on the grill for 30 seconds, turning once, just to warm.

Cover the inside of each pita with the tahini spread. Add the mixed vegetables and sliced meat. Serve immediately.

Makes 6 to 8 servings.

Peanut Butter–Banana
on Date-Nut Bread

A *lmost a dessert, this unusual combination of ingredients is* *one of my favorite sandwiches. The white cabbage adds a pleasing crunch and texture.*

Combine the peanut butter and jalapeño pepper.

Spread peanut butter on 6 slices of bread and cover with preserves. Arrange banana slices over the preserves and top with shredded cabbage. Cover each with a second slice of bread. Press to secure the ingredients.

Makes 6 servings.

1 cup natural chunky
  peanut butter
1–2 small red jalapeño
  peppers, minced
1 cup blueberry preserves
2 bananas, sliced
  very thin
½ small head white
  cabbage, shredded fine
12 fairly thin slices
  Date-Nut Bread
  (see page 30)

Sardines and Canadian Bacon with
Egg on Toasted Whole Wheat Bread

A *hearty sandwich inspired by Portuguese cuisine. Typically,* *fish, meat, and eggs are combined to create a powerful taste sensation.*

Spread a thin layer of mustard on each slice of bread. Arrange half the greens on 6 slices of the bread, then the Canadian bacon, egg, and sardines. Top with the remaining greens and cover with a second slice of bread.

Makes 6 servings.

COOK'S NOTE:

Use an assortment of bitter greens or just one. Choose from escarole, endive, radicchio, arugula, frisée, curly endive, dandelion greens, or watercress. For extra mustard flavor, try mustard greens.

¼ cup Hot-Pepper
  Coarse-Grained
  Mustard (see page 10)
12 slices whole wheat
  bread, toasted
1 bunch bitter greens
  (see COOK'S NOTE)
6 slices Canadian bacon
6 hard-boiled eggs,
  sliced thin
2 cans oil-packed
  sardines, drained

Pan Bagna

A traditional Italian sandwich, doused with good olive oil and filled with wonderful ingredients. Pressing the sandwich with heavy weights produces a chewy, slightly moist bread. The olive oil and juice from the tomatoes soak through the bread, spreading good flavors as they go.

1 large round of Italian or sourdough French bread, halved horizontally

⅔ cup fruity olive oil

1 medium red onion, sliced thin

2 tins anchovies, chopped

2 medium tomatoes, sliced medium thick

Black pepper

⅔ cup oil-cured olives, pitted and chopped

⅔ cup ripe green olives, pitted and chopped

2 large red peppers, roasted, peeled, and seeded

Brush the cut sides of the bread with olive oil. You can be generous with the oil because it soaks into the bread as it stands.

Layer the onion on the bottom piece of the bread, cover with the anchovies and tomatoes and sprinkle with black pepper. Sprinkle the olives over the tomatoes and top with the peppers. Cover with the top half of the bread and wrap in plastic. Place a cutting board or large flat object on the sandwich. Weight it with heavy books, cans, or a large pot filled with water. Make sure the entire sandwich is being pressed. Allow the weighted sandwich to stand at room temperature for at least 4 hours. Unwrap and slice.

Makes 6 to 8 servings.

Roast Lamb with Fried Garlic on Rosemary Fougasse

A simple and elegant sandwich with plenty of character. Use elephant garlic if possible for this dish—its flavor is milder and sweeter than that of the regular variety. Bulbs or "heads" of elephant garlic are huge, so you may not need a whole one.

Preheat oven to 450° F.

Brush the lamb with olive oil and sprinkle with black pepper. Place the lamb on a rack in a greased roasting pan. Roast the meat for 30 to 35 minutes or until the desired doneness is achieved. Remove the lamb from the oven and let rest at room temperature.

Peel the cloves of garlic with a paring knife. If the cloves are difficult to peel, soak them in very hot water for 2 or 3 minutes to make the skins easier to remove. Slice the cloves as thinly as possible. Cook the garlic in the butter, 2 tablespoons olive oil, and the mustard seed over low heat until the garlic is tender, about 15 minutes.

Cut the bread into 6 squares and slice through the middle to make top and bottom pieces for sandwiches. Spread a thin layer of Honey Mustard on the bottom pieces.

Arrange some rocket on the mustard; top with a slice of tomato and slivers of garlic. Slice the lamb and layer it over the tomato. Place with a second slice of tomato on the meat and cover with bread.

Makes 6 servings.

2½ pounds boneless lamb tenderloin, trimmed of fat
Olive oil
Freshly cracked black pepper
Garlic cloves from 1 head elephant garlic or 2 heads regular garlic
2 Tb. unsalted butter
1 Tb. yellow mustard seed

1 recipe Rosemary Fougasse (see page 19)
Honey Mustard (see page 11)
1 bunch rocket
12 slices tomato

Roast Pepper and Hot Coppa on Pumpkin-Spice Bread

*S*picy and savory coppa, sweet peppers, and spicy pumpkin bread make for a unique and delicious sandwich. This sweet and hot sandwich is so easy and fast to make, it requires almost no work! Bake the bread a day ahead as it is better the day after it is baked.*

1 Tb. olive oil

1 clove garlic

¾ pound hot coppa, sliced very thin (see COOK'S NOTE)

1 bunch rocket, leaves only

12 slices Pumpkin-Spice Bread (see page 32)

2 large peppers, roasted, peeled, and seeded

Heat the olive oil in a skillet, add the garlic and coppa, and cook just to heat through, about 30 seconds. Remove from the pan and set aside.

Arrange the rocket on 6 slices of the bread, cover with the coppa, and top with slices of pepper. Arrange a few more pieces of rocket on top of the pepper and cover with a second piece of bread.

Makes 6 servings.

COOK'S NOTE:

Hot coppa is cured or cooked pork shoulder rolled in black pepper, dried and then cured. The result is slightly salty, spicy, flavorful meat. If you prefer a more subtle taste, use mild coppa, which is not rolled in black pepper. These delicious meats are available at Italian delis or gourmet food markets.

Janet's Childhood Favorite

This was my favorite sandwich as a child. Trying this "recipe" again convinced me that some things stay with you no matter what. This is a good sweet-sour sandwich not only for kids, but for those who will forever be kids at heart.

Spread the peanut butter on 6 slices of the bread, top with the potato chips and then the pickles. Spread the jam on the other 6 slices of bread. Put the jam slice on the peanut butter slice and press to crush the potato chips.

Makes 6 servings.

1 cup natural chunky
  peanut butter
12 slices whole wheat
  bread
6 or 8 dill pickles,
  sliced thin
1–1½ cups thick
  potato chips
¾ cup apricot jam

Warm and Melted Sandwiches

These sandwiches range from hot to barely warm and many include cheese, which is melted under a broiler or in a hot oven. I feel that no food has to be so painfully hot that you cannot taste it. As long as the ingredients are warm all the way through or the cheese has melted, the sandwiches will be fine. Remember that unwrapped bread warmed in the oven for more than three minutes can become dry. Serve melted cheese sandwiches as soon as you remove them from the oven because cold (melted) cheese becomes rubbery.

Grilled Salmon with Chili-Mint Mayonnaise and Pickled Onions on Toasted Sesame Roll

MARINADE
½ cup sesame oil
¼ cup dry sherry
1 clove garlic, minced
1 Tb. crushed red
  peppercorns

6 salmon fillets

**CHILI-MINT
MAYONNAISE**
1 cup Mayonnaise
  (see page 12)
⅓ cup minced fresh mint
1 small red jalapeño
  pepper, seeded and
  minced
1 1-inch piece fresh
  ginger, peeled and
  minced
Juice of 1 lime
Salt and pepper, to taste

½ cup seasoned rice wine
  vinegar
1 cup water
2 Tb. black peppercorns
2 bay leaves
4 cloves garlic, sliced thin
2 small red onions, peeled
  and sliced thin

6 sesame rolls, halved and
  toasted
1 head butter lettuce

*T*his light and refreshing sandwich is as pleasing to look at as it is to eat. If a grill is unavailable, use a broiler. The whole thing takes just minutes to assemble once the individual components are made.

Combine the marinade ingredients and pour over the salmon. Place the fish and marinade in a large heavy plastic bag and seal. This method ensures that the fish will stay immersed in the marinade. Marinate at room temperature for 2 hours.

Combine the mayonnaise with the remaining Chili-Mint Mayonnaise ingredients; mix well. Taste and adjust the seasoning. Refrigerate the aioli until you are ready to use it.

Heat the vinegar, water, peppercorns, bay leaves, and garlic in a small saucepan. When the mixture comes to a boil, remove from the heat and pour over the onions. Allow the onions to cool at room temperature. Onions thus prepared can be stored at room temperature for about 2 weeks.

Prepare a charcoal grill.

When the coals are red hot, place the salmon on the grill. Cook 2 minutes per side, brushing with the marinade. Remove the salmon from the grill and set aside.

Spread the bottom of each roll with a little mayonnaise, place lettuce leaves over the mayonnaise and salmon over the lettuce. Put about 1 tablespoon of mayonnaise and one-sixth of the onions on top of the salmon. Cover with the tops of the rolls and serve immediately. Makes 6 servings.

Grilled Duck with Apple-Apricot Chutney on California Walnut Bread

A *good sandwich for brunch or a light lunch. The sweet chutney is the perfect companion for rich and flavorful duck. If duck is unavailable, dark meat of chicken may be substituted.*

Cook the onion, garlic, chili pepper, and spices in the olive oil and butter over high heat for 2 minutes, stirring constantly. Reduce the heat and cook until the onion is soft. Add the apple, raisins, apricots, and lime juice; cook over moderate heat until the fruit is tender when pierced with a fork, about 15 to 20 minutes. Season with salt and pepper. Let chutney cool to room temperature.

Prepare a charcoal grill. A broiler can be used if a grill is unavailable.

Rub the duck breasts with olive oil and black pepper. When the coals are hot, place the duck on the grill and cook until done, about 3 to 5 minutes, depending on the size of the duck and heat of the coals. Remove the duck from the grill, discard its skin and slice the meat into thin strips.

Spread each piece of bread with a little butter. Place the greens on 6 pieces of bread and top with chutney. Place the duck over the chutney and cover with a second piece of bread. Serve immediately.

Makes 6 servings.

COOK'S NOTE:

Choose from any of these bitter greens: escarole, curly endive, endive, radicchio, arugula, watercress, dandelion greens, or mustard greens for a mustardy taste.

CHUTNEY
1 yellow onion, diced small
1 clove garlic, minced
1 serrano chili pepper, minced
1 tsp. mustard seed
½ tsp. each, coriander, anise seed, fennel seed, and ground cardamom
2 Tb. olive oil
2 Tb. unsalted butter
1 large green apple, peeled and cored, diced small
½ cup golden raisins
5 dried apricots, diced small
Juice of 3 limes
Salt and pepper, to taste

6 small or 3 large boned half duck breasts
Olive oil
Black pepper

12 slices California Walnut Bread (see page 34)
Unsalted butter (optional)
1 bunch bitter greens, shredded or torn into small pieces (see COOK'S NOTE)

Grilled Flank Steak, Pinto Bean Spread, and Feta Cheese with Corn Tortillas

This satisfying and hearty sandwich can be eaten in the hands or open-faced on a plate. The meat is tender and spicy, the beans sharp and smoky. Feta cheese adds an unusual tang.

PINTO BEAN SPREAD
1 cup pinto beans, washed and sorted
4 cups water
2 bay leaves
2 slices bacon
1 large onion, diced small
3 cloves garlic, minced
2 jalapeño peppers, minced
1 Tb. ground coriander
1 tsp. oregano
3 Tb. bacon fat
3 Tb. olive oil
⅓ cup red wine
2 Tb. sherry vinegar
¼ cup minced cilantro
Salt and pepper, to taste

MARINADE
⅔ cup olive oil
½ cup tomato paste
Juice of 3 limes
3 cloves garlic, minced
1 Tb. each, dry oregano, sage, ground cumin, and thyme
2 tsp. black pepper

2 pounds flank steak
12 Corn Tortillas (see page 35)
¾ pound feta cheese, crumbled
2 tomatoes, diced small
Cilantro sprigs for garnish

Cook the pinto beans in the water and bay leaves until very tender. Allow the beans to sit in the cooking liquid until cool; remove the bay leaves and drain. Mash with a fork until fairly smooth.

Cook the bacon until golden brown and crisp. Remove it from the fat and set aside. Discard all but 3 tablespoons of the fat. When the bacon is cool, chop it fine.

Cook the onion, garlic, jalapeño peppers, coriander, and oregano in the 3 tablespoons of bacon fat and olive oil over low heat until the onion is soft, about 8 minutes. Add the wine and cook until it has evaporated. Remove from the heat and add to the mashed pinto beans; mix well. Add the vinegar, cilantro, reserved bacon, salt, and pepper; taste and adjust the seasoning. Set the spread aside at room temperature until you are ready to use it.

Combine the marinade ingredients; mix well. Spread the marinade over the meat. Place the meat and marinade in a baking pan and marinate in the refrigerator overnight or at room temperature for 3 hours.

Prepare a charcoal grill (see COOK'S NOTE).

When the coals are very hot, place the meat on the grill. Cook, flipping frequently, until the meat is done, about 3 minutes for each inch of thickness on each side. Length of cooking time depends on how long the meat was marinated, heat from the coals, thickness of the meat, and how you like your meat cooked. Remove the cooked meat from the grill, keeping in mind that it will continue to cook for a few minutes. Allow it to rest for 5 minutes before cutting. Slice it across the grain as thinly as possible.

Place the tortillas on the grill for about 1 minute, just to warm.

Spread some of the pinto bean mixture on a warm tortilla, add some sliced meat, sprinkle with cheese, and top with diced tomato. Fold in half and garnish with cilantro.

Makes 6 servings.

COOK'S NOTE:

If an outdoor grill is unavailable, broil the steak and warm the tortillas in an oven. To warm the tortillas, simply wrap the stack in tinfoil and place in a low oven for 4 or 5 minutes; serve immediately.

Grilled Fish with California Combo on Onion Fougasse

*R**ipe and creamy avocados and melted cheese are a combination that make this one of my favorite sandwiches. Onion rolls may be used in place of Onion Fougasse.*

6 firm fish fillets, such as
   halibut, swordfish,
   tuna, or shark
Olive oil
White pepper
1 dried ancho or pasilla
   pepper, seeded and
   soaked for 1 hour
¾ cup Mayonnaise
   (see page 12)
1 small red onion,
   diced small
2 Tb. chopped dill pickle
2 Tb. capers
Pinch of cayenne
Salt and pepper, to taste

Onion Fougasse
   (see page 19)
6 slices tomato
6 slices Monterey Jack
   cheese (about ½ pound)
2 ripe avocados, sliced

COOK'S NOTE:

If a charcoal grill is unavailable, bake the fish in
an oven. Place the fish fillets in a shallow baking
pan, roast at 400° F until
tender and springy to the
touch, top with cheese, and
cook until the cheese melts.

Coat the fish fillets with olive oil and sprinkle with white pepper. Let the fish rest at room temperature for about 1 hour.

Meanwhile, purée the ancho pepper with a little of the soaking liquid until smooth. Add to the mayonnaise and mix well. Add the onion, pickle, capers, and cayenne; mix well. Season with salt and pepper.

Just before cooking the fish, spread some sauce on both pieces of the roll. Place a slice of tomato on the bottom portion of the roll; set aside.

Prepare a charcoal grill (see COOK'S NOTE).

When the coals are hot, place the fish on the grill and cook on one side about 2 minutes. Flip the fillets and place a slice of cheese on top of each piece; cook for 3 minutes or until the cheese has melted. Remove from the grill and place on onion rolls, top with avocado, and serve immediately.

Makes 6 servings.

Smoked Turkey with Cumin Slaw and Melted Gouda Cheese on Light Orange-Carrot Rye

S moked turkey and spicy slaw make a juicy and tasty sandwich. Gouda cheese is full flavored without being overpowering and rounds out the combination perfectly.

Preheat oven to 450° F.

Combine the cabbage, onion, garlic, green pepper, cumin, caraway seed, mayonnaise, and vinegar in a large bowl; mix well. Season with salt and pepper.

Place about 3 tablespoons of slaw on 6 slices of the bread. Place the turkey over the slaw and top with two slices of cheese. Place under a broiler and heat until the cheese melts. Cover with a little more slaw and a second slice of bread. Serve immediately.

Makes 6 servings.

1 small head red cabbage, shredded
1 small onion, sliced thin
1 clove garlic, minced
1 small green pepper, slivered
1 tsp. cumin seed
½ tsp. caraway seed
¾ cup Mayonnaise (see page 12)
3 Tb. apple cider vinegar
Salt and pepper, to taste

12 slices Light Orange-Carrot Rye sliced diagonally (see page 25)
1 pound smoked turkey, sliced thin
1 pound imported Gouda cheese, cut into 12 thick slices

Potato Galette and Swiss Raclette with Cornichons and Caramelized Onions

This rich fork-and-knife sandwich will be very popular. Golden brown potatoes, flavorful cheese, and sweet and sour onions are accented by tart cornichon pickles. Make two separate galettes. Who says sandwiches have to be served on bread?

PEARLS

2 Tb. unsalted butter

15 to 20 pearl onions, trimmed and peeled

¾ cup red wine

1 tsp. sugar

2 Tb. red wine vinegar

Salt and pepper, to taste

FOR 2 GALETTES

2 Tb. unsalted butter

4 cloves garlic, minced

5 large white potatoes, peeled and sliced ⅛ inch thick

2 Tb. oregano

1 Tb. fresh thyme

½ tsp. ground fresh rosemary

3 Tb. all-purpose flour

1 cup chicken stock

Salt and pepper, to taste

¾ pound Swiss raclette cheese, grated

½ cup chopped cornichons (see COOK'S NOTE)

Watercress for garnish

Melt the butter in a heavy sauté pan. Add the onions and cook over high heat for 5 to 7 minutes, stirring constantly. Add the wine and sugar and cook over high heat for 3 minutes. Reduce the heat and continue to cook until the onions are soft, but still intact, about 30 minutes. Add the vinegar and cook until all the liquid has evaporated. Season with salt and pepper. Cool to room temperature.

Make the first galette by melting half the butter in a 10-inch skillet. Add 2 cloves of the garlic and cook for 1 minute over moderate heat. Add half the potatoes, layering them in a circle around the skillet (see Figs. 1 and 2, page 65). Sprinkle with half the herbs. Cook over high heat for 1 to 2 minutes, reduce the heat, and add 1½ tablespoons flour and ½ cup chicken stock, salt, and pepper. Cook over moderately high heat, covered, for 10 to 15 minutes. Do not stir or move the potatoes. When they are tender, increase the heat and cook, uncovered, for 1 or 2 minutes. Slide the potatoes from the skillet in one piece onto a plate.

Make the second galette.

Return one galette to the skillet. Lay some of the onions on top of the potatoes; cover with the cheese and cornichons. Place the galette under a broiler and melt the cheese. Cover with the second galette, gently pressing to secure the ingredients. Place the galette under the broiler for 2 to 3 minutes to brown slightly. Cut the galette into 4 or 6 wedges. Remove it from the pan with care because the galette will be soft and delicate. Serve immediately on a bed of watercress.

Makes 4 to 6 servings.

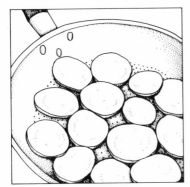 

Fig. 1 Layer the pan with potato slices.

Fig. 2 Continue adding the potatoes until you have several layers forming the galette.

COOK'S NOTE:

Cornichons, small French pickles often served with paté, have a pleasant, tart flavor. Most gourmet food shops and many supermarkets carry these imported pickles.

Pita with Curried Lamb, Feta Cheese, and Spinach

Delicious aromas will fill the air as the curried lamb cooks. A moist and tender filling is sparked with tangy feta cheese and bright green spinach. Make sure the pita bread is fresh; otherwise it tears easily.

¼ cup fruity olive oil
2½ pounds lamb
   shoulder, cut into
   ½-inch pieces
¼ cup red wine
2 medium onions,
   diced small
3 cloves garlic, minced
2 small dried hot red chili
   peppers, crushed
1 Tb. ground coriander
1 tsp. each, ground
   cumin, anise,
   fenugreek, mace,
   turmeric, mustard
   seeds, and black
   pepper
½ tsp. cardamom
1½ cups peeled and
   chopped tomatoes
2 cups beef stock
1 red pepper, diced small
Salt and pepper, to taste

6 pita breads, halved
½ pound imported feta
   cheese, crumbled
1 small bunch spinach,
   washed and stemmed

Heat half the olive oil in a large sauté pan. When the oil is hot but not smoking, add the lamb and cook over high heat for 3 to 5 minutes or until golden brown on all sides. Remove the meat from the pan with a slotted spoon and set aside. Deglaze the pan with the wine.

In the remaining oil, cook the onions, garlic, chili peppers, and all the spices over high heat for 2 to 3 minutes, stirring constantly. Add the tomatoes, lamb, and stock and cook over high heat for 3 minutes. Reduce the heat and cook over low heat until the lamb is very tender, about 1 hour. Add the red pepper, mix well. Season with salt and pepper.

Fill each pita pocket with curried lamb. Tuck 4 or 5 spinach leaves into the side of the pocket and garnish with feta cheese. Serve immediately.

Makes 6 servings.

Sardines, Onion, and Mustard Greens on Toasted Black Bread

S omehow this seems like a "man's" sandwich—not because it is large, full of meat, or filling, but because I've never met a man in any part of the world who didn't like sardines. I know that every one of you who hates sardines will write to me. At any rate, the sandwich has a big taste.

Cook the onions and garlic in the butter over high heat until golden brown, about 5 minutes. Stir often to prevent burning. Season with pepper. Keep warm until you are ready to use it.

Spread Honey Mustard on 6 slices of the bread, placing mustard greens over each. Top with the onions and sprinkle with some niçoise olives. Lay 4 or 5 sardines (depending on the size) over the onions and olives; drizzle with lemon juice. Cover with mustard greens and top with a second slice of bread.

Makes 6 servings.

2 yellow onions,
   sliced thin
2 cloves garlic, minced
2 Tb. unsalted butter
Freshly cracked black
   pepper, to taste

Honey Mustard
   (see page 11)
1 small bunch mustard
   greens, washed,
   stemmed, and chopped
   medium
12 slices Black Bread
   (see page 24), toasted
⅔ cup niçoise olives,
   pitted and chopped
2 cans sardines, packed in
   oil and slightly drained
Juice of 2 lemons

Scrambled Eggs with Chinese Sausage and Peppers on Chili Bread Cheese Toast

*M*y friend Lee suggested Chinese sausages for this dish. I think they are marvelous little flavor packets, crisp, succulent, and quite different from Italian sausages. You can find them at Asian markets.

6 Chinese sausages, cut into 1-inch pieces
1 Tb. olive oil
1 onion, diced medium
1 tsp. fennel seed
⅓ cup dry white wine
1 small red pepper, diced small
1 small green pepper, diced small

⅓ pound sharp Cheddar cheese, grated
¼ pound Italian fontina cheese, grated
12 slices Chili Bread (see page 23)

8 large eggs, lightly beaten
⅓ cup minced fresh chives
2 Tb. minced cilantro
Salt and pepper, to taste

Cook the sausages in the olive oil over low heat for 2 minutes. Remove the sausage with a slotted spoon and set aside. Add the onion, fennel seed, and wine and cook over moderate heat until the onion is soft and the wine has evaporated. Add the peppers and cook over high heat for 1 minute, stirring constantly. Remove them from heat and set aside in the sauté pan.

Preheat oven to 400° F.

Mix the cheeses and distribute on the 12 slices of bread. Place the bread on cookie sheets and heat in the oven until the cheese starts to melt. Meanwhile, heat the sausage, onion, and peppers over moderate heat for 1 minute. Add the eggs and cook over moderate heat until they are almost set. Add the herbs, salt, and pepper. Remove the cheese bread from the oven. Place the eggs on six slices of the cheese bread. Cover them with a second slice of cheese bread and serve immediately.

Makes 6 servings.

Muffuletta

This is a lusty sandwich from the equally lusty French Quarter in New Orleans. Make one large sandwich and set it aside for 2 to 3 hours. The flavors and ingredients soak into the bread, creating a hearty and tasty meal. A lively green salad would be a good companion.

Brush both cut sides of the bread with the olive oil. Sprinkle the olives over the bottom half of the bread. Layer the meats and cheese over the olives. Season with black pepper. Cover with the top half of the bread. Press to secure the ingredients. Place a heavy weight on top of the sandwich and allow it to "rest" at room temperature for 2 to 4 hours.

Slice into wedges and serve.

Makes 6 to 8 servings.

1 large round Italian bread, or 6 small round rolls, halved horizontally

⅔ cup fruity olive oil

1 cup black olives, pitted and chopped

⅓ pound salami, sliced

⅓ pound mortadella, sliced

½ pound smoked ham, sliced

⅔ pound provolone cheese, sliced

Freshly cracked black pepper

English Melt on Flour Tortilla

This simple and elegant sandwich uses delicate flour tortillas for "holders." A good port makes a nice accompaniment to this almost classic combination of Stilton cheese and walnuts.

Divide the cheese among 6 of the tortillas. Top with rocket and sprinkle with walnuts. Cover with the remaining tortillas.

Melt the butter with the olive oil in a large skillet. Add the tortilla sandwiches and cook over low heat until light golden brown, but not crisp. Carefully flip the sandwiches and cook until the tortillas and cheese are soft, about 1 minute. Remove the sandwiches from the pan, cut them into quarters, and serve immediately.

Makes 6 servings.

1 pound English Stilton, crumbled

12 small flour tortillas

1 large bunch rocket, washed and stemmed

1¼ cups toasted walnuts, chopped coarsely

2 Tb. unsalted butter

1 Tb. olive oil

Fried Oysters and Corn-Pepper Tartar Sauce on Warm French Rolls

*C*rispy *on the outside and tender on the inside, oysters and French bread are sauced with a colorful and zesty tartar sauce. A new twist on the traditional Poor Boy sandwich. I use oysters from a jar that are plump, fresh and delicious. Of course you can shuck your own if you have the time.*

CORN-PEPPER TARTAR SAUCE

1 cup Mayonnaise (see page 12)

3 Tb. red pepper, diced small

1 green onion, minced

1 ear uncooked corn, shaved

1 Tb. capers

1 Tb. chopped pickle

1 Tb. minced fresh parsley

Salt and pepper, to taste

1 cup–plus all-purpose flour

½ cup fine cornmeal

½ tsp. each, dry oregano, basil, thyme

1 cup vegetable oil

8 to 12 raw oysters

6 French rolls, halved

Horseradish Mustard (see page 12)

1 bunch arugula, washed and stemmed

Combine all the ingredients for the Corn-Pepper Tartar Sauce in a bowl; mix well. Taste and adjust the seasoning.

Mix the flour, cornmeal, and herbs. Coat the oysters with the mixture and set them aside.

Heat the oil in a large skillet. When the oil is hot, but not smoking, add the oysters and cook in batches until golden brown. Drain on paper towels.

Meanwhile, heat the rolls in a warm oven. When they are heated through, spread each piece with a thin layer of mustard and top with tartar sauce. Cover the bottoms of the rolls with arugula, oysters, and the tops of the rolls. Serve immediately.

Makes 6 servings.

Pan Con Chumpe

*R*oast turkey, crisp vegetables, and a peanuty sauce make up
this traditional El Salvadoran sandwich. It's a flavor-packed
meal, complete with vegetables, meat, and bread.

Soak the ancho peppers in water to cover for 2 to 3 hours, or
until the peppers are soft. Remove the seeds and stems. Set
aside.

Cook the onion, garlic, and oregano in the olive oil over
moderate heat for 10 minutes, stirring often. Add the tomatoes,
cinnamon, and spices. Cook over high heat for 3 minutes. Reduce the heat and cook over moderate heat for 15 minutes or
until the tomatoes are soft and mushy. Transfer the mixture to a
blender and add the ancho peppers. Purée to a smooth sauce.
Strain the sauce through a fine wire mesh to remove the tomato
seeds and skins. Place the sauce in a pan, add the peanut butter,
and mix well. Cook the sauce over low heat for 10 to 15 minutes.
Season with salt and pepper. Keep the mixture warm over low
heat.

Place turkey on the bottom halves of the rolls and spoon
warm sauce over it. Arrange the radishes, cucumber, and lettuce
on the turkey and cover with the tops of the rolls. Serve immediately.

Makes 6 servings.

SAUCE
2 ancho peppers
1 medium onion, small
 diced
4 cloves garlic, minced
1 tsp. oregano
¼ cup olive oil
6 tomatoes, chopped
1 cinnamon stick
1 tsp. ground coriander
½ tsp. mace
3 rounded Tb. natural
 peanut butter
Salt and pepper, to taste

2–2½ cups roast turkey,
 preferably dark meat
6 French or Italian rolls,
 halved
6 radishes, sliced thin
18 medium slices
 cucumber
Lettuce

Bacon-Teleme Melt on Maple-Pecan Bread

1 pound bacon
12 thin slices Maple-Pecan Bread (see page 31)
1 pound teleme cheese, sliced (see COOK'S NOTE)

*I*t is hard to imagine that this simple combination of only three ingredients can make an absolutely great sandwich, but nothing could improve it. The subtle taste of maple and bacon are reminiscent of some favorite breakfast moments.

Preheat broiler to 500° F.

Cook the bacon until golden brown and crisp. Drain on a paper towel. Cover the bread with the cheese. Place under the broiler and heat until the cheese melts and is slightly bubbly. Remove the bread from the broiler and top 6 slices with the bacon. Put the remaining slices over them to make closed sandwiches.

Make 6 servings.

COOK'S NOTE:

Teleme is a soft, sometimes runny, Jack cheese. You can substitute the firmer Jack, but it doesn't have the same character.

Ham, Bitter Greens, and Melted Brie on Date-Nut Bread

1 bunch rocket, watercress, or escarole, washed and stemmed
12 slices Date-Nut Bread (see page 30)
1 pound smoked ham, sliced thin
¾ pound imported Brie cheese, cut into small pieces

*R*ich and creamy brie cheese and smoky ham are delightful companions for sweet dates and bitter greens. A simple sandwich that is assembled very quickly.

Preheat broiler to 500° F.

Arrange the greens on 6 slices of the bread. Layer the ham over the greens and cover evenly with the cheese. Place under the broiler and heat just until the cheese barely melts. Cover with a second slice of bread and serve immediately.

Baked Sandwiches

B aked sandwiches are cozy and comforting. Most are good with a cup of hot soup on a cold day. I like the idea of sitting around a big table with friends, drinking beer and chomping on oversized, warm sandwiches toasty from the oven.

In most cases these sandwiches use bread as their base. Heat them long enough to melt the cheese or to heat the ingredients through to the middle. Prolonged heating in the oven causes the bread to dry. All the separate components must be cooked and ready to eat because the baking does not cook the food but only warms it. Baked sandwiches are good for those who are limiting their fat intake because no oil or butter is required in the cooking or heating process. An outdoor grill can be a substitute for an oven.

Baked Ham, Tilsit, and Dill Pickle on Black Bread

A warm and comforting sandwich that goes beautifully with dark beer. Easy to prepare and assemble.

⅔ cup Hot-Pepper Coarse-Grained Mustard (see page 10)
12 slices Black Bread (see page 24)
12 slices Tilsit cheese, about ¾ pound
1 cup thinly sliced dill pickles
1½ pounds baked ham, sliced thin

Preheat oven to 300° F.

Spread mustard on each slice of bread. Cover 6 of the slices with 1 slice of cheese. Layer with pickles, ham, and the remaining cheese. Cover with a second slice of bread.

Bake for 15 minutes or until the cheese is soft and the ingredients are hot. Serve immediately.

Makes 6 servings.

Baked Italian Melt with Pesto

A garlic lover's sandwich that oozes with melted cheese and pesto. Make the pesto a day ahead to cut down on preparation time. My mouth waters when I think about this sandwich.

Preheat oven to 400° F.

Place all the pesto ingredients in a blender and blend for 2 minutes to a smooth paste, scraping the sides of the blender from time to time. Add a little water if necessary to thin the pesto. Taste and adjust the seasoning.

Spread each piece of roll with pesto and place some arugula on all pieces. Layer the red peppers, coppa, and artichokes on 6 of the pieces. Press firmly to secure the ingredients. Top with cheese.

Place the rolls in the oven and bake until the cheese has melted and the ingredients are warm. Top with a second piece of roll and serve immediately.

Makes 6 servings.

PESTO
- 2 bunches basil, washed and stemmed
- 2 cloves garlic
- ½ cup grated Parmesan cheese
- ¼ cup pine nuts
- ⅔ cup olive oil
- Salt and pepper, to taste

- 6 soft Italian rolls, halved
- 1 bunch arugula, washed and stemmed
- 3 large roasted red peppers, peeled, seeded, and medium sliced
- 1½ pounds hot coppa, sliced thin (see COOK'S NOTE on page 54)
- 2–3 jars marinated artichoke hearts, drained and halved
- 1 pound mozzarella cheese, sliced medium

Prosciutto, Figs, and Orange with Port Butter on Toasted Brioche

This is a perfect sandwich for brunch or a light lunch. It is just as good to look at as it is to eat! The slightly salty meat combines very well with the sweet figs and the refreshing taste of the orange.

¾ cup port wine
¼ pound unsalted butter, lightly whipped

6 brioches, halved and toasted (see COOK'S NOTE)
¾ pound prosciutto, sliced very thin
9 fresh Black Mission figs, halved
1 large orange, sectioned
Cracked pepper

Preheat oven to 350° F.

Place the port in a small saucepan and cook over high heat until it is reduced to a thick syrup. Allow to cool slightly. Add to the butter; mix well.

Spread the butter on all the pieces of brioche and cover with prosciutto. Top 6 of the brioche halves with 2 or 3 pieces of fig and 2 sections of orange. Season with black pepper. Cover with the remaining brioche halves. Bake for 3 minutes, just to warm the ingredients. Serve immediately.

Makes 6 servings.

COOK'S NOTE:

Brioche is a heavenly French egg bread baked in the shape of a mushroom. It has a buttery, eggy flavor and is excellent toasted. Challah or any good egg bread may be substituted. A delicious brioche can be made from the recipe on page 32.

Smoked Ham with
Yam Spread and Currants on
Light Orange-Carrot Rye

The yam spread is yummy on its own, but when it is combined with smoky ham and crisp green beans the result is heavenly. Be sure to cut the sandwich in half to expose the bright green "stripes."

Preheat oven to 350° F.

Cook the yams in salted boiling water until tender, about 20 to 25 minutes. Drain and cool. Mash with a fork. Set aside in a bowl.

Cook the onion, apple, and spices in the butter until the onion is soft and the apple is crisp-tender. Add the onion-apple mixture, currants, and maple syrup to the yams; mix well. Season with salt and pepper.

Spread each slice of bread with yam spread. Arrange 4 string beans on 6 slices of the bread and top with the ham. Cover with a second slice of bread.

Bake for 3 to 5 minutes, just to warm through. Serve immediately.

Makes 6 servings.

2 small or 1 large yam, peeled and coarsely chopped
1 medium onion, diced small
1 green apple, peeled and diced small
1 tsp. ground coriander
Pinch each, mace, cinnamon, cayenne
5 Tb. unsalted butter
½ cup currants
2 Tb. pure maple syrup
Juice of 1 lemon
Salt and pepper, to taste

12 slices Light Orange-Carrot Rye
(see page 25)
24 string beans, blanched
1 pound smoked ham, sliced thin

Grilled Sausage with Pepper-Onion Sauté on Italian Roll

*C**lassic and simple, this traditional sandwich needs no formal introduction.*

2 large onions, sliced
  medium
4 cloves garlic, minced
½ tsp. each, dry oregano,
  basil, and thyme
1 Tb. yellow mustard
  seed
⅓ cup olive oil
1 red pepper, sliced
  medium
1 green pepper, sliced
  medium
1 California chili, or any
  slightly hot green
  pepper, sliced thin
Salt and pepper, to taste
6 sweet Italian sausages
Tomato-Herb Mustard
  (see page 11)
1 pound provolone
  cheese, sliced medium
  thick
6 Italian rolls, halved

Preheat oven to 400° F. Prepare a charcoal grill.

Cook the onions, garlic, spices, and mustard seed in the olive oil over high heat for 3 to 5 minutes, stirring often. Add the peppers and cook over low heat until the peppers are tender, but not soft. Season with salt and pepper. Set aside.

When the coals are hot, place the sausages on the grill. Cook the sausages, rotating often, until done, about 7 to 10 minutes, depending on how hot the coals are.

In the meantime, spread a thin layer of mustard on the bottom part of each roll. Place the cheese on each of the 12 halves of roll. Heat them in the oven until the cheese is bubbly. Put some pepper-onion mixture and then a sausage on the 6 bottom halves. Cover them with tops of the rolls.

Makes 6 servings.

Stilton Cheese and Pear-Walnut Chutney with Port Butter on French Baguette

An elegant and unusual sandwich. Served with a glass of port or sherry, it becomes a delightful lunch offering. The port butter is a beautiful mauve color.

Preheat oven to 350° F.

Cook the onion and spices in the butter over low heat until the onion is soft. Add half the apple juice and cook over moderate heat for 1 minute. Add the pears and cayenne and cook over moderate heat for 3 minutes. Add the remaining apple juice and cook until the pears are tender, but not mushy. Remove from the heat and cool. Add the walnuts; mix well. Season with salt and pepper. Set aside at room temperature.

Cook the port in a small saucepan over high heat until the wine is reduced to a thick syrup. Cool slightly and add to the whipped butter; mix well.

Spread the port butter on both sides of the baguette. Place the greens over the butter. Spoon chutney onto the bottom half of the baguette and top with the cheese. Cover with the other half of the baguette. Heat in the oven for 3 to 5 minutes, just to warm through. Cut into serving sizes and serve immediately.

Makes 6 servings.

1 small onion, diced small
¼ tsp. each, ground coriander, cardamom, mace, turmeric, fennel seed, and black pepper
2 Tb. unsalted butter
1 cup apple juice
2 firm pears, peeled, cored, and diced small
Pinch cayenne
½ cup toasted walnuts, chopped medium
Salt and pepper, to taste
¾ cup port wine
¼ pound unsalted butter, lightly whipped

1 or 2 French baguettes, sliced lengthwise
1 bunch arugula (see COOK'S NOTE)
1 pound English Stilton cheese, sliced

COOK'S NOTE:

Arugula, also called rocket, has a nutty, slightly bitter flavor, perfect for this sandwich. You may substitute any slightly bitter green such as baby romaine, frisée, watercress, or mild green such as butter lettuce, red or green leaf lettuce.

Tomato with Five-Olive Paste on Rosemary Fougasse

*M*editerranean ingredients make this sandwich a robust and flavor-packed lunch offering. Serve a full-bodied red wine and a mixed green salad to complete the meal.

FIVE-OLIVE PASTE
1 medium onion, diced
  small
3 Tb. olive oil
⅓ cup each, niçoise,
  Calamata, oil-cured,
  green, and California
  black olives, pitted
  and chopped
1 tsp. thyme
4 prunes, minced
1 Tb. balsamic vinegar
Splash of sherry vinegar
1 clove garlic, minced
2 anchovies, minced
Salt and black pepper,
  to taste

1 recipe Rosemary
  Fougasse, cut into
  12 equal squares or
  rectangles (see page 19)
½ cup fruity olive oil
1 bunch rocket, trimmed
  and washed
12 slices tomato

Preheat oven to 350° F.

Cook the onion in the olive oil over low heat until the onion is soft. Place in a bowl. Add the olives, thyme, prunes, vinegars, garlic, and anchovies. Season with salt and pepper.

Brush the top of the fougasse with a little fruity olive oil. Arrange the rocket on 6 pieces of the bread; add olive paste and tomato slices. Cover with a second piece of fougasse. Bake for 5 minutes. Serve immediately.

Makes 6 servings.

Spicy Ratatouille with Bel Paese on Sourdough Roll

*S*ourdough rolls are excellent holders for thick and spicy ratatouille. Melted Italian cheese makes this filling and nutritious
vegetarian sandwich irresistible.

Preheat oven to 350° F.

Cook the mushrooms in 2 tablespoons olive oil in a large
sauté pan over high heat until golden brown, stirring often. Set
aside.

Cook the onions, garlic, spices, and hot peppers in ⅓ cup
olive oil over moderate heat until the onions are soft. Add the
eggplant and cook over high heat for 1 minute. Add the tomatoes, reduce the heat, and cook over low heat until the eggplant
is almost tender, about 15 minutes. Add the zucchini, red pepper, olives, and reserved mushrooms; cook until all the vegetables are tender, but not mushy. Season with salt and pepper.

Spoon ratatouille onto the bottom half of each roll and top
with cheese. Bake for 7 to 10 minutes, or until the cheese has
melted. Cover with the tops of the rolls and serve immediately.

Makes 6 servings.

½ pound mushrooms,
  sliced thick
⅓ cup plus 2 Tb. olive oil
2 medium onions, diced
  small
3 cloves garlic, minced
1 tsp. each, dry oregano,
  basil, thyme, and sage
2 dry hot red peppers,
  crushed
1 eggplant, diced small
1 28-ounce can peeled and
  seeded whole tomatoes
1 zucchini, diced small
1 red pepper, diced small
½ cup oil-cured olives,
  pitted and chopped
Salt and pepper, to taste

6 sourdough rolls, halved
  and toasted
1 pound imported Bel
  Paese, 12 slices (see
  COOK'S NOTE)

COOK'S NOTE:

Bel Paese is a mild,
slightly tart Italian cow's
milk cheese that is deli-
cious plain and excellent
for cooking. The domestic
Bel Paese is quite good,
but I favor the imported. If
this cheese is unavailable,
substitute Tellegio or Italian or Swedish fontina.

Bacon, Turkey, and Tomato with Peanut-Raisin Cream Cheese on French Bread

*S*alty, *sweet, and nutty flavors combine to make an unusual sandwich. The ingredients may sound peculiar, but the tastes and textures work very well together.*

1 pound natural cream
 cheese, softened
½ cup roasted peanuts,
 chopped
⅓ cup raisins
1 pound bacon

12 slices country-style
 French bread, toasted
12 slices tomato
1 pound turkey,
 sliced thin

Preheat oven to 350° F.

Combine the cream cheese, peanuts, and raisins in a bowl; mix well. Set aside at room temperature.

Cook the bacon until crisp and drain on paper towels.

Spread some cream cheese on the bread. Arrange the bacon on 6 of the bread slices. Top with tomato slices and turkey. Cover with a second piece of bread. Heat in the oven for 3 to 5 minutes, just to warm. Serve immediately.

Makes 6 servings.

Grilled Sandwiches

I love grilled sandwiches. Those oh-so-greasy grilled cheese sandwiches oozing with Velveeta or American cheese are stuck in my memory, and probably in my gut. Somehow, even *those* tasted good! The grilled sandwich recipes that follow hardly compare with those of yesteryear, and the use of oil or grease is kept to a minimum. Use only enough to soak into the bread and turn it a golden brown.

Of course, a grilled sandwich is not made on a grill (over coals) but on a griddle or in a pan. For more on grilling and griddling, refer to the Basic Techniques section, pages 5–7. If you are trying to cut down on fat consumption, serve these sandwiches baked or warmed. They definitely taste better grilled, but since the ingredients remain the same, the end result is good no matter what.

Grilled Italian Meats with Feta and Marinated Green Beans on Pumpernickel

A sandwich for meat and garlic lovers. The combination of meats goes well with the feta cheese. Grilling the sandwich adds a delicious olive oil taste and makes the bread slightly crunchy. The green beans add a surprise taste and color in the center of the sandwich.

MARINADE
½ cup olive oil
¼ cup white wine vinegar
2 cloves garlic, minced
1 red jalapeño pepper, sliced very thin
½ tsp. each, dry oregano, basil, thyme, and black pepper
Salt, to taste

½ pound green beans, trimmed and blanched
¾ pound feta cheese, 12 slices
12 slices pumpernickel
½ pound turkey, sliced thin
½ pound ham, sliced thin
½ pound mild coppa, sliced thin (see COOK'S NOTE on page 54)
Olive oil, for grilling

Combine the marinade ingredients and pour over the green beans. Marinate the beans for at least 4 hours at room temperature or overnight in the refrigerator.

Arrange the cheese on 6 slices of the bread. Top with the turkey, then the ham. Place the green beans over the meat; cover with coppa and a second slice of bread. Press to secure the ingredients.

Heat 2 to 3 tablespoons of olive oil in a sauté pan or on a griddle. Cook the sandwiches over low heat until golden brown on one side. Carefully flip the sandwiches and cook until the second side is golden brown, using more olive oil if necessary. Feta cheese does not get runny as it cooks, so the sandwiches should be done when the bread is golden brown and the ingredients are warm.

Makes 6 servings.

Grilled Cheddar and Turkey with Sweet Pickles and Tomato on Oatmeal Bread

*O*atmeal bread is a tender holder for this irresistible sandwich oozing with sharp cheese. The sweet pickles add tang and cut the richness of the cheese and butter. Whole wheat bread will also work well.

Spread a thin layer of mustard on 6 slices of the bread and arrange half the cheese over the mustard. Top with the pickles, turkey, tomato, and remaining cheese. Cover with a second slice of bread. Press firmly to secure the ingredients.

Melt the clarified butter in a sauté pan or on a griddle. Cook the sandwiches over low heat until golden brown on one side. Carefully flip the sandwiches and cook until the second side is golden brown. Serve immediately.

Makes 6 servings.

Tomato-Herb Mustard
  (see page 11)
12 slices oatmeal bread
1 pound Canadian
  Cheddar cheese, sliced
1 cup thinly sliced sweet
  pickles
1 pound turkey breast,
  sliced thin
6 large tomato slices

4 Tb. clarified butter
  (see page 5)

Grilled Eggplant and Mozzarella with Roast Peppers on Sun-Dried Tomato Brioche

2 Japanese eggplants,
   sliced into ½-inch-thick
   ovals
⅔ cup olive oil
Salt and pepper, to taste
¾ cup balsamic vinegar
1 pound mozzarella
   cheese, sliced thin with
   serrated knife

12 slices Sun-Dried
   Tomato Brioche
   (see page 33)
1 bunch arugula, washed
   and stemmed
3 large roasted red
   peppers, peeled,
   seeded, and sliced
   medium
Freshly cracked black
   pepper
Olive oil, for grilling

COOK'S NOTE:

The vinegar reduces quickly, so keep an eye on it. When it begins to get thick, remove it from the heat. If the reduction hardens while the eggplant is baking, simply add a tablespoon of fresh vinegar to it and stir. Use it immediately.

A full-flavored vegetarian sandwich, good with cold beer or red wine.

Preheat oven to 400° F.

Grease a large cookie sheet. Arrange the sliced eggplant on the cookie sheet, brush generously with the olive oil, and sprinkle with salt and pepper. Bake for 15 to 20 minutes, until the eggplant is tender, but not mushy.

Meanwhile, place the balsamic vinegar in a small saucepan and cook over high heat until the vinegar is reduced to a thick syrup (see COOK'S NOTE). When the eggplant is done, brush it with the vinegar reduction. Set the eggplant aside to cool.

Arrange half the cheese on 6 slices of the bread and place arugula over the cheese and roasted peppers over that. Sprinkle with black pepper. Top with the eggplant and the remaining cheese; cover with a second slice of bread.

Heat 2 to 3 tablespoons olive oil in a sauté pan or on a griddle. Cook the sandwiches over low heat until golden brown on one side. Carefully flip the sandwiches and cook until the second side is golden brown. Serve immediately.

Makes 6 servings.

Grilled Lamb and Tomato with Roquefort Cheese on Pita Rounds

*T*he lamb is so tender and tasty, you may be tempted to eat it before making the sandwich. But do resist! The final product is better.

Combine the marinade ingredients; mix well. Pour over the lamb and marinate overnight in the refrigerator or for 3 hours at room temperature.

Combine the cheeses, butter, garlic, and pine nuts; mix well. Season with pepper.

Prepare a charcoal grill.

When the coals are red hot, remove the lamb from the marinade and place it on the grill. Cook the lamb about 15 minutes or until done (see COOK'S NOTE). Remove it from the grill and set aside. When it is cool enough to handle, slice into thin pieces.

Spread some roquefort mixture on each piece of pita. Arrange the tomatoes on top of 6 pieces of the bread. Cover with the sliced meat and top with a second piece of bread with cheese. Heat 2 to 3 tablespoons oil in a sauté pan or on a griddle. Cook the sandwiches over low heat until the pita bread is slightly crisp and barely golden brown on both sides. Slice each of the six round sandwiches into quarters and serve immediately.

Makes 6 to 8 servings.

MARINADE
1¼ cups olive oil
½ cup red wine
3 Tb. tomato purée
3 cloves garlic, minced
½ tsp. each, dry oregano, basil, and ground coriander

2–2½ pounds lamb tenderloin
¼ pound roquefort cheese
¼ pound natural cream cheese, softened
3 Tb. unsalted butter, softened
1 clove garlic, minced
½ cup toasted pine nuts
Black pepper, to taste

12 small (5-inch) pieces pita bread
18 small slices tomato
⅓ cup minced fresh parsley
Olive oil, for grilling

COOK'S NOTE:

Cooking time depends on the heat of the coals, marinating time, thickness of the meat, and the degree of doneness you prefer.

Grilled Chicken, Mushroom, and Cheese on Egg Bread

6 large half chicken
  breasts
1 cup white wine
4 cups chicken stock
2 bay leaves
1 tsp. black peppercorns
2 Tb. unsalted butter
2 Tb. olive oil
1½ pounds mushrooms,
  chopped fine
2 Tb. mushroom soy
  sauce
3 Tb. Coarse-Grained
  Hot-Pepper Mustard
  (see page 10)
Black pepper, to taste

12 slices Egg Bread
  (see page 20)
12 slices Danish fontina
  cheese, about 1¼
  pounds
12 slices tomato
Clarified butter, for
  grilling (see page 5)

COOK'S NOTE:

It is important to cook the
mushrooms in two batches
so they sear rather than
steam. This requires a lot
of room and high heat.

Tender chicken, meaty mushrooms, and melted cheese make this sandwich a true star. Serve it on a cold day with a cup of rich tomato soup and diners will be delighted.

Place the chicken breasts in a large skillet. Add the wine, chicken stock, bay leaves, black peppercorns, and water to cover. Bring the mixture to a boil, reduce the heat to low, and simmer until the meat is springy to the touch and white all the way through, about 10 to 15 minutes. Do not overcook. Remove the chicken from the liquid and set it aside. When it is cool enough to handle, remove the chicken from the bones and cut it into ½-inch strips, taking care to remove any fat or cartilage.

Heat 1 tablespoon each of the butter and oil in a large sauté pan. When the butter has melted, add half the mushrooms and cook over high heat, stirring often until all the liquid has evaporated (see COOK'S NOTE). Add half the mushroom soy sauce and mix well. Remove the mushrooms from the pan and set aside. Cook the remaining mushrooms following the same procedure, and add to the first batch. Add mustard and black pepper to the mushrooms and mix well.

Cover each of 6 slices of the bread with a slice of cheese, top with 2 tablespoons mushroom mixture, chicken, tomato, and a second slice of cheese. Cover each with a second slice of bread. Press to secure ingredients.

Heat a thin layer of clarified butter in a sauté pan or on a griddle. When medium hot, cook the sandwiches until golden brown on one side. Carefully flip the sandwiches and cook until the second side is golden brown. Serve immediately.

Makes 6 servings.

Reuben Sandwich

*T**he classic Reuben asks for little if any alteration. Cold beer and potato salad are great companions. Having grown up on the East Coast, I remember Reubens on rye. Some people may prefer black bread. The orange and carrot rye makes this traditional sandwich a bit different.*

Combine all the Russian dressing ingredients in a bowl; mix well. Taste and adjust the seasoning.

Spread 6 slices of the bread with a thin layer of mustard. Spread all 12 slices with the Russian Dressing. Place the meat on 6 slices of the bread and top with cheese and sauerkraut. Cover with a second slice of bread.

Heat a thin layer of clarified butter in a large sauté pan or on a griddle. When the butter is hot, cook the sandwiches until golden brown on one side. Carefully flip the sandwiches and cook until the second side is golden brown. Serve immediately.

Makes 6 servings.

RUSSIAN DRESSING
¾ cup Mayonnaise (see page 12)
3 Tb. chili sauce
1½ Tb. chopped pickle
1½ Tb. chopped onion
1 Tb. grated horseradish
Salt and pepper, to taste

12 slices Light Orange-Carrot Rye (see page 25)
Horseradish Mustard (see page 12)
1½ pounds corned beef, sliced thin
12 slices imported Swiss cheese (Emmenthaler)
1 cup sauerkraut, drained
Clarified butter, for grilling (see page 5)

Philly Cheese Steak

*A**ll the ingredients in this sandwich are grilled together and the cheese is melted right on top of the peppers, onions, and meat. Making this dish is similar to stir-frying, except that the food is cooked on a flat surface. It's fast and easy to prepare.*

Heat the oil in a large sauté pan or on a griddle. When the oil is hot, but not smoking, add the onions and cook over high heat for 3 minutes, stirring often. Add the flank steak and cook about 2 minutes. Add all the peppers and cook for 1 to 2 minutes, stirring constantly. Season with salt and pepper. Reduce the heat and cover the meat and vegetables with the grated cheese.

When the cheese has melted, place the mixture between the two halves of the rolls. Serve immediately.

Makes 6 servings.

3 Tb. olive oil
2 onions, sliced medium
½ pound flank steak, sliced thin across the grain
1 red pepper, sliced medium
1 green pepper, sliced medium
6 hot cherry peppers, sliced medium
1 pound sharp Cheddar cheese, grated
Salt and pepper, to taste

6 Italian rolls, halved

Grilled Polenta and Vegetable Ricotta Filling with Pancetta Tomato Sauce

This filling fork-and-knife sandwich is large and complex enough to serve for dinner. Add a green salad and garlic bread for a satisfying meal.

POLENTA
3 cups water
2 cloves garlic, minced
3 Tb. unsalted butter
1¼ cups coarse yellow cornmeal
¼ tsp. nutmeg
Salt and pepper, to taste

PANCETTA TOMATO SAUCE
⅓ pound pancetta, minced
1 large onion, diced small
2 cloves garlic, minced
½ tsp. each, basil, oregano, and thyme
⅓ cup red wine
15 fresh or 1 28-ounce can tomatoes, chopped
Salt and pepper, to taste

Bring the water, garlic, and butter to a boil in a medium saucepan. Slowly add the cornmeal, stirring constantly. When all the cornmeal has been added, reduce the heat to low and cook, uncovered, for 15 to 20 minutes, stirring often. The mixture should be thick and creamy. Add the nutmeg, salt, and pepper. Taste and adjust the seasoning. Pour the polenta into a 9-by-12-inch baking dish. Spread the polenta to the edges and smooth the surface. Brush the surface with oil to prevent drying. Cover with plastic wrap and refrigerate for 6 hours or overnight. When the polenta is set, cut it into 3-by-3-inch squares. Remove them from the pan and set aside.

Cook the pancetta in a large skillet until golden brown. Remove it with a slotted spoon and set aside. Cook the onion, garlic, and herbs in the fat remaining in the skillet over low heat until the onion is soft. Add the wine and cook over high heat for 2 minutes, stirring constantly. Add the tomatoes and cook over high heat for 3 minutes, stirring often. Reduce the heat and cook over moderate heat until the tomatoes are soft, 15 to 20 minutes. Cool slightly. Purée in a blender until smooth. Strain the sauce through a fine wire sieve. Return the strained sauce to the pan and add the reserved pancetta. Cook over moderate heat until the sauce is thick. Season with salt and pepper. Keep warm over low heat.

Combine the cheeses, zucchini, red pepper, and spices; mix well. Add the sun-dried tomatoes and stir just enough to mix. (Sun-dried tomatoes will turn the mixture pink if they are over-mixed.) Season with salt and pepper.

Place the filling on 6 pieces of the polenta. Top with a second piece of polenta; press gently to secure.

Heat a thin layer of olive oil in a large sauté pan or on a griddle. Cook the polenta sandwiches over moderate heat until golden brown on one side, about 5 minutes. Carefully flip the sandwiches and cook until the second side is golden brown.

Spoon some sauce onto each plate and place a sandwich in the center. Garnish with sprigs of flat leaf parsley.

Makes 6 servings.

FILLING
1 pound fresh ricotta cheese
¼ pound Parmesan cheese, grated fine
¼ pound Italian fontina cheese, grated
1 small zucchini, diced small
1 small red pepper, diced small
¼ tsp. each, mace, cardamom, and cinnamon
⅓ cup sun-dried tomatoes, minced
Salt and pepper, to taste

Olive oil, for grilling
Flat leaf parsley, for garnish

Grilled Three-Jewel Cheese Spread with Chicken on Spice Bread

The filling for this special sandwich can be made a day ahead, leaving just the grilling for the last minute.

THREE-JEWEL CHEESE SPREAD

½ pound natural cream cheese, softened

½ pound sharp white Cheddar cheese, grated

1 tsp. each, cumin and caraway seed

½ tsp. ground coriander

1 medium zucchini, diced small

1 large red apple, diced small

½ cup chopped roasted peanuts

Pinch cayenne

4 large half chicken breasts

1 cup white wine

3 cups chicken stock

2 bay leaves

1 tsp. black peppercorns

12 slices Spice Bread (see page 20)

Clarified butter, for grilling (see page 5)

Combine all the ingredients for the cheese spread in a large bowl; mix well. Taste and adjust the seasoning. Set aside at room temperature.

Place the chicken breasts in a large pot. Add the wine, chicken stock, bay leaves, and black peppercorns. Bring the mixture to a boil and immediately reduce the heat to low. Simmer for about 20 minutes, or until the chicken is springy to the touch and white all the way through. Do not overcook the chicken. Remove it from the poaching liquid. When it is cool enough to handle, remove the skin, bones, and any cartilage or fat and cut into small pieces. Add to the cheese mixture.

Spread the chicken-cheese mixture on 6 slices of the bread; then cover with the remaining bread. Press to secure ingredients.

Heat a thin layer of clarified butter in a sauté pan or on a griddle. Cook the sandwiches over moderate heat until golden brown on one side. Carefully flip the sandwiches and cook until the second side is golden brown. Serve immediately.

Makes 6 servings.

Croque Vivienne

This delightfully simple sandwich works because of a few tasty ingredients. Veal is the traditional meat used for this French sandwich, but boned chicken breasts may be substituted.

Combine the bread crumbs, ½ cup of flour, and the herbs. Place in a shallow bowl and set aside.

Dredge the veal cutlets in the remaining flour. Dip into the egg, drain slightly, and dip immediately into the bread crumb mixture. Make sure the meat is fully coated with crumbs. When all the meat has been breaded, refrigerate for 15 minutes.

Heat about 4 tablespoons vegetable oil in a large skillet. When the oil is hot, add the cutlets in batches and cook over moderate heat until golden brown on both sides. Drain on paper towels.

Arrange half the cheese on 6 slices of the bread, top with a veal cutlet, and drizzle with lemon juice. Cover with a second piece of cheese and top with a second slice of bread. Press to secure ingredients.

Heat a thin layer of clarified butter in a sauté pan or on a griddle. Cook the sandwiches, covered, over low heat until golden brown on one side. Carefully flip the sandwiches and cook until the second side is golden brown and the cheese has melted. Serve immediately.

Makes 6 servings.

1 cup dry (fine) bread crumbs

1 cup all-purpose flour

½ tsp. each, dry oregano, basil, sage, and black pepper

6 small veal cutlets, trimmed and pounded very thin

2 large eggs, lightly beaten

Vegetable oil, for cooking

12 slices Gruyère cheese, about 1 pound

12 slices seedless rye bread

Juice of 2 lemons

Clarified butter, for grilling (see page 5)

Croque Monsieur

This classic French treat, with a small twist, makes a satisfying brunch or lunch offering.

1 pound Emmenthaler cheese, grated

⅓ cup heavy cream

¾ cup cornichons, patted dry and minced

Tomato-Herb Mustard (see page 11)

12 slices Spice Bread (see page 20)

12 thick slices ham

4 large eggs, lightly beaten

Clarified butter, for grilling (see page 5)

Combine the cheese, cream, and cornichons. Spread a thin layer of mustard on 6 slices of the bread. Spread cheese mixture on all 12 slices. Place the ham on 6 of the bread slices. Top each with a second slice of bread. Dip each sandwich into the beaten egg.

Heat half the butter in a sauté pan or on a griddle. Cook the sandwiches, covered, over low heat until golden brown on one side. Add the remaining butter. Carefully flip the sandwiches and cook until the second side is golden brown. Serve immediately.

Makes 6 servings.

Jamaican Fried Egg Sandwich

T his sandwich can be made at any time of the year, but I en-
joyed it under the hot, sultry August sun in Negril, Jamaica.
Basic ingredients jazzed up with hot peppers and cabbage make
a great snack.

Combine the cabbage, onion, green pepper, garlic, jalapeño pepper, and cumin seed with the mayonnaise; mix well. Add the hot
sauce, and season with salt and pepper.

Cover each slice of bread with a slice of cheese. Place a slice
of tomato on 6 slices of the bread and top each with a fried egg
and slaw. Cover the slaw with a second slice of bread. Press to
secure ingredients.

Heat a thin layer of clarified butter in a sauté pan or on a
griddle. Cook the sandwiches over low heat until golden brown
on one side. Carefully flip the sandwiches and cook until the second side is golden brown, adding more butter as necessary.
Serve immediately.

Makes 6 servings.

1½ cups white cabbage,
  shredded fine
1 small white onion,
  sliced thin
½ green bell pepper,
  slivered
1 clove garlic, minced
1 red jalapeño pepper,
  minced
1 tsp. cumin seed
¾ cup Mayonnaise
  (see page 12)
Dash hot sauce
Salt and pepper, to taste

12 slices whole wheat
  bread
12 slices Cheddar cheese
6 large slices tomato
6 large eggs, fried
Clarified butter, for
  grilling (see page 5)

Sandwich Cubano

A traditional Cuban sandwich combines two full-flavored meats and crisp dill pickles. To make this as authentic as possible, you must use only butter and no mayonnaise.

¼ pound unsalted butter, softened

6 French rolls, halved

¾ pound Swiss cheese, sliced

¾ pound roast pork, shredded

¾ cup dill pickles, sliced thin

¾ pound ham, sliced thin

Clarified butter, for grilling (see page 5)

Spread butter on the cut side of each roll. Layer half the cheese on the bottom portions of the rolls. Top with the roast pork, pickles, and ham. Cover with the remaining cheese and top halves of the rolls.

Melt some clarified butter in a large skillet. Cook the sandwiches over low heat, placing a weight on top of the sandwiches or pressing with a spatula to flatten as they cook, until golden brown on one side. Flip and cook until the second side is golden brown and the cheese has melted.

Makes 6 servings.

Open-Face Sandwiches

Bread isn't the only vehicle for sandwich fillings, as the following recipes show. Many are sophisticated fork-and-knife sandwiches. Served with a salad and condiments, several of these dishes are appropriate for company. Even though these sandwiches are made with only one piece of bread or with no bread at all, most are substantial.

Vegetable-Potato Frittata with Olive Cream Cheese

A *perfect brunch or breakfast meal for egg and olive lovers. Since all the ingredients are cooked in one pan, the mixture requires little attention once it goes into the oven. Warm muffins or bread are good with the frittata.*

2 potatoes, diced small
1 yellow onion, diced small
¼ cup olive oil
⅓ cup white wine
1 zucchini, diced small
1 red pepper, diced small
½ cup diced ham
3 Tb. minced mixed fresh herbs
Pinch red pepper flakes
10 large eggs, lightly beaten
¾ pound natural cream cheese, softened
2 Tb. each, pitted and chopped ripe green, California black, niçoise, and Calamata olives
1 tsp. dry thyme
1 clove garlic, minced
Black pepper, to taste
Mixed greens (see COOK'S NOTE)
Basic Vinaigrette (recipe on page 99)

Cook the potatoes in salted boiling water until tender when pierced with a fork. Drain and cool.

Preheat oven to 350° F.

Cook the onion in olive oil in a 10-inch nonstick skillet over moderate heat for 5 minutes. Add the wine and cook over low heat until the onion is soft. Add the zucchini, pepper, ham, herbs, and red pepper flakes and cook over high heat for 1 minute, stirring constantly. Add the potatoes and mix well.

Add the eggs and cook over moderate heat, stirring constantly, until the eggs begin to set. Smooth the surface of the eggs and place them in the oven. Bake for 20 to 30 minutes or until the eggs are completely set. Remove them from the oven and set aside. When the eggs are completely cool, remove them from the pan and set aside.

Combine the cream cheese, olives, thyme, garlic, and black pepper in a bowl. Taste and adjust the seasoning.

Spread the olive cream cheese over the top of the frittata. Cut it into wedges and place them on a bed of greens dressed with vinaigrette. Serve at room temperature.

Makes 6 to 8 servings.

Whisk the vinegar into the olive oil so that it forms an emulsion. Add the garlic, salt, and pepper.

BASIC VINAIGRETTE
½ cup olive oil
3 Tb. sherry vinegar
1 clove garlic, minced
Salt and pepper, to taste

COOK'S NOTE:

Choose any variety of greens such as frisée, watercress, mustard greens, rocket, butter lettuce, mâche, or romaine. I like to mix mild and bitter flavors, but any combination is appropriate.

Roast Duck, Plum-Apricot Jam, and Watercress on Fried Noodle Rounds

This spicy jam will find its way to your table time and time again because it goes well with poultry, meat, and many different cheeses. Buy a delicious roast duck in an Asian market, specialty shop, or gourmet food store or roast your own.

1 or 2 fresh ducks, depending on size, or 2½ cups cooked duck meat

Black pepper

PLUM-APRICOT JAM

⅓ cup chopped dried apricots

5 firm plums, pitted, peeled, and chopped (see COOK'S NOTE)

1 2-inch piece fresh ginger, minced

2 jalapeño peppers, minced

2 Tb. sugar

½ cup water

Preheat oven to 500° F.

Puncture the skin of the duck with the tines of a fork. Rub pepper on the skin. Place the duck on a rack in a greased roasting pan. Place in the oven and cook for 5 minutes at 500° F. Reduce the heat to 300° F and roast for 2½ hours, or until the meat is cooked all the way through. Remove from the oven and let stand. When the duck is cool enough to handle, remove all the meat from the bones, taking care to remove the fat and cartilage. Shred the meat into bite-size pieces.

Combine all the ingredients for Plum-Apricot Jam in a nonreactive saucepan. Bring the mixture to a boil, reduce the heat, and cook over low heat until the fruit is soft and the mixture thick, about 20 to 25 minutes. Taste and adjust the sugar. Jam should not be too sweet.

COOK'S NOTE:

To make them peel easier, drop plums into boiling water for 30 seconds, remove, and plunge into cold water. Peel.

Cook the noodles in salted boiling water until just tender, taking care not to overcook. Drain and cool the noodles. Combine with the green onions, garlic, five-spice powder, black bean sauce, salt, pepper, eggs, and sesame oil; mix well. Taste and adjust the seasoning. Heat half the vegetable oil in an 8-inch nonstick skillet, add half the noodle mixture, and cook over moderate heat until golden brown on the bottom. Carefully flip the noodle pancake over and cook until the second side is golden brown (see illustration below). Set aside. Cook the second pancake with the remaining noodle mixture, following the same procedure. Set aside.

Cut the pancakes into wedges. Arrange some of the watercress on top of the pancakes, top with the jam, and finish with smoked duck. Serve at room temperature or warm.

Makes 6 to 8 servings.

Cook noodle rounds until golden brown on both sides.

NOODLE ROUNDS

- ½ pound very thin egg noodles, such as spaghettini
- ¾ cup minced green onions
- 4 cloves garlic, minced
- 1 tsp. Chinese Five-Spice Powder (see page 14)
- 3 Tb. black bean sauce (see COOK'S NOTE)
- Salt and pepper, to taste
- 3 large eggs, lightly beaten
- ⅓ cup cold-pressed sesame oil
- Vegetable oil, for cooking

- 1 large bunch watercress, washed and stemmed

COOK'S NOTE:

Black bean sauce in jars is available at Asian markets and many large supermarkets.

Barbecued Pork with Marinated Green Beans on Corn Bread

2-pound pork loin, rolled
  and tied
Olive oil
Black pepper

BARBECUE SAUCE
6 slices bacon
1 large yellow onion,
  chopped
3 cloves garlic, minced
½ tsp. each, ground
  oregano, coriander,
  fennel, cayenne,
  mustard seeds, cumin,
  and black pepper
¼ cup apple cider vinegar
¼ cup soy sauce
2 Tb. hot-sweet mustard
12 medium tomatoes,
  chopped
⅓ cup brown sugar

MARINATED BEANS
¼ pound yellow wax
  beans, trimmed and
  cut
  on the diagonal into
  ½-inch pieces
¼ pound green beans,
  trimmed and cut on the
  diagonal into ½-inch
  pieces
¼ cup olive oil
1 Tb. seasoned rice wine
  vinegar
1 clove garlic, minced
4 large radishes, diced
  small
Salt and pepper, to taste

1 recipe Corn Bread
  (see page 29)

*S*erve the juicy roast pork and its spicy sauce over tender Corn Bread. Make the sauce and bread a day ahead to simplify preparation.

Preheat oven to 500° F.

Rub the pork with olive oil and sprinkle with black pepper. Insert a meat thermometer in the center of the pork. Place the meat on a rack in a greased roasting pan. Place in the oven and cook for 5 minutes at 500° F. Reduce the heat to 350° F and roast about 20 minutes for each pound, or until the thermometer reads 155° F. Remove the pork from the oven and allow it to cool at room temperature. When cool enough to handle, slice the pork into thin pieces; set aside, covered.

To make the Barbecue Sauce, cook the bacon in a heavy skillet until crisp. Remove it with a slotted spoon. Save 3 tablespoons of bacon fat and discard the rest. Crumble the bacon into small pieces. Cook the onion, garlic, and spices in the bacon fat over low heat for 7 minutes. Add the vinegar, soy sauce, and mustard and cook over moderate heat for 1 minute, stirring constantly. Add the tomatoes and cook over high heat for 1 minute, then add the brown sugar and reserved bacon. Reduce the heat and cook for about 1 hour, stirring often to prevent sticking. Cool slightly. Strain the sauce through a fine sieve or food mill. The sauce should be smooth and thick. Taste and adjust the seasoning.

Blanch the beans in salted boiling water for 1 minute. Plunge the beans into ice water, then drain them. Combine the remaining marinade ingredients in a nonreactive bowl; mix well. Add the beans, mix well, and marinate overnight in the refrigerator or for 3 hours at room temperature. Taste and adjust the seasoning.

Place a large piece of Corn Bread on each plate. Arrange slices of pork on the bread, spoon hot sauce over the meat, and garnish with marinated beans. Serve immediately.

Makes 6 to 8 servings.

Roast Pork, Smoked Cheese, and Tomato Salsa on Navajo Fry Bread

Preheat oven to 500° F.

Rub the pork with olive oil, garlic, salt, and pepper. Insert a meat thermometer into center of meat. Place the meat on a rack in a greased roasting pan and cook in the oven for 5 minutes. Reduce the heat to 325° F and roast 30 minutes to the pound, or until the thermometer reads 155° to 165° F. Remove from the oven and allow to cool slightly.

Combine the tomatoes, corn, onion, peppers, cilantro, salt, and pepper in a nonreactive bowl; mix well. Taste and adjust the seasoning; set aside at room temperature.

Top the Navajo fry bread with cheese, chunks of roast pork, and tomato salsa.

Makes 6 to 8 servings.

2½ pounds pork tenderloin, to yield 2 cups shredded roast pork
Olive oil
4 cloves garlic, minced
Salt and pepper

TOMATO SALSA
2 ripe tomatoes, diced medium
¾ cup fresh corn kernels
1 small onion, diced small
1 to 2 jalapeño peppers, minced
¼ cup chopped cilantro

¾ pound natural smoked cheese, such as Bruderbasil, grated
2 recipes Navajo Fry Bread (see page 36)

1 large roasting chicken

2 Tb. bacon fat

2 Tb. Chinese Five-Spice
Powder (see page 14)

3 cloves garlic, minced

1 2-inch piece ginger,
peeled and minced

2 tsp. black pepper

CURRY MAYONNAISE

1 cup Mayonnaise
(see page 12)

¼ tsp. each, ground
coriander, fennel seed,
fenugreek, anise seed,
cumin seed, and black
pepper

Pinch each, cayenne,
nutmeg, and mace

2 cloves garlic, minced

¼ cup minced green
onions

Salt and pepper, to taste

1 small daikon, peeled
and sliced very thin
(see COOK'S NOTE)

¼ pound green beans,
sliced thin on the
diagonal

2 Tb. toasted sesame oil

2 Tb. seasoned rice wine
vinegar

Salt and pepper, to taste

1 recipe Navajo Fry
Bread (see page 36)

¼ cup black sesame
seeds, for garnish

Cilantro sprigs, for
garnish

Five-Spice Chicken, Daikon, and Curry Mayonnaise on Navajo Fry Bread

Preheat oven to 450° F.

Truss the chicken for roasting. Make a paste of the bacon fat, five-spice powder, garlic, ginger, and black pepper; mix well. Rub the chicken with the paste. Place the chicken on a rack in a greased roasting pan and cook for 5 minutes. Reduce the heat to 350° F and roast about 20 minutes per pound, or until the juices run clear. Remove from the oven. When the chicken is cool enough to handle, remove all the meat from the carcass, taking care to remove the fat, tendons, and cartilage. Set aside.

Combine the mayonnaise, spices, garlic, green onions, salt, and pepper. Taste and adjust the seasoning.

Combine the daikon, green beans, sesame oil, and rice wine vinegar. Season with salt and pepper.

Spread mayonnaise on 6 pieces of Navajo fry bread, top with chicken, and finish with daikon and beans. Garnish with black sesame seeds and cilantro.

Makes 6 servings.

COOK'S NOTE:

Daikon is a Japanese radish. It is long, firm, and creamy white and, like the familiar red radish, it is spicy and peppery. Red radishes may be substituted for daikon.

Grilled Flank Steak, Gorgonzola, and Greens on Navajo Fry Bread

*T**his is a very rich dish, and Gorgonzola fans will rejoice.*

Combine the marinade ingredients and pour over the steak. Marinate overnight in the refrigerator or for 3 hours at room temperature. Be sure the meat is covered with the marinade at all times.

Prepare a charcoal grill.

When the coals are red hot, place the meat on the grill and cook 4 to 5 minutes per side or until the meat is done to your liking. Length of cooking time depends on the thickness of the meat, marinating time, heat from the coals, and how you like your meat cooked. Remove the meat from the grill and set aside until it is cool enough to handle. Slice as thinly as possible, across the grain, and set aside, covered.

Arrange watercress and arugula on 6 pieces of Navajo fry bread, top with slices of steak, and dot with small pieces of cheese. Garnish with pistachio nuts.

Makes 6 servings.

MARINADE
1 cup olive oil
½ cup red wine
2 Tb. Dijon mustard
2 Tb. mushroom
    soy sauce
2 cloves garlic, minced
½ tsp. each, sage, thyme,
    basil, savory, rosemary,
    and black pepper

2 pounds flank steak

1 or 2 recipes Navajo Fry
    Bread (see page 36)
1 small bunch arugula,
    washed and stemmed
1 small bunch watercress,
    washed and stemmed
¾ pound imported
    Gorgonzola cheese
½ cup toasted
    pistachio nuts

Risotto Squares with Grilled Tuna, Spinach, and Sesame-Garlic Butter

Risotto is a rich and creamy Italian rice dish. Try to resist eating it immediately, or you won't have enough left for the recipe. The fried squares make an irresistible base for tender grilled tuna. An elegant and filling dish.

RISOTTO SQUARES

4 Tb. unsalted butter

1 small onion, diced small

3 cloves garlic, minced

½ tsp. each, thyme, basil, and ground coriander

1 tsp. red pepper flakes

1½ cups Arborio rice

5 cups chicken stock

¼ cup small-diced carrot

¼ cup small-diced zucchini

¼ cup small-diced red pepper

⅓ pound Italian fontina cheese, grated

3 Tb. grated Parmesan cheese

Salt and pepper, to taste

Olive oil, for cooking

Melt the butter in a heavy saucepan. Cook the onion, garlic, herbs, and spices over moderate heat until the onion is soft. Add the rice and cook over high heat, stirring constantly, for 1 minute. Add 1 cup of the chicken stock, stir well, and reduce the heat to low. Cook the risotto, stirring often, until the stock has been absorbed. Add a second cup of stock and cook until it has been absorbed, stirring often. Continue with the remaining stock, 1 cup at a time, until the rice is creamy and tender. Then add the carrot, zucchini, red pepper, cheeses, salt, and pepper; mix well. Cook over low heat just long enough to melt the cheese, about 3 minutes. Taste and adjust the seasoning. Remove from the heat and spoon into a lightly greased 9-by-11-inch baking dish; smooth the rice to the edges and corners. Cover and refrigerate for at least 4 hours. When cold, cut into 6 squares and carefully remove from the pan and set aside.

To prepare the sesame-garlic butter, melt 1 tablespoon of the butter in a skillet. Add the garlic and cook over moderate heat until it is golden brown and crispy. Set aside in a bowl. Combine the remaining 4 tablespoons of butter with the sesame seeds, chives, and cooked garlic; mix well. Season with salt and pepper.

Heat a thin layer of olive oil in a large nonstick skillet. When the oil is hot, but not smoking, add the risotto squares in batches and cook over high heat until golden brown on one side. Flip the rice squares very carefully and cook until the second side is golden brown, adding oil if necessary. Keep warm in a low oven while you cook the fish.

Prepare a charcoal grill.

Coat each fillet with sesame oil. When the coals are hot, place the fish on the grill and cook about 1½ minutes on each side. *Do not overcook*. Remove the fish from the grill and assemble immediately (see COOK'S NOTE).

In a large skillet, cook the spinach, using only the water clinging to the leaves. Cook over high heat until the spinach just wilts, about 30 seconds. Set aside.

Place a risotto square on each of 6 plates, arrange some spinach on top of each square, cover with a fish fillet, and garnish with sesame-garlic butter. Serve immediately.

Makes 6 servings.

SESAME-GARLIC BUTTER

5 Tb. unsalted butter
12 cloves garlic, chopped
2 Tb. toasted
    sesame seeds
2 Tb. minced fresh chives
Salt and pepper, to taste

3 fresh tuna fillets, about
    ½ to ¾ pounds each,
    sliced in half through
    the center
Toasted sesame oil
1 bunch spinach, washed
    and stemmed

COOK'S NOTE:

It is most important that the fish be served right off the grill, still hot. The sesame-garlic butter should melt slightly as the dish is served. Warming the plates before serving helps.

Potato Cakes with Smoked Salmon and Dill Crème Fraîche

*T*hese cakes are made with cooked and mashed potatoes rather than the traditional grated potatoes. They are delicious with an assortment of foods.

TOMATO CONCASSE
3 ripe tomatoes, peeled, seeded, and diced small
1 Tb. olive oil
1 Tb. vodka
Salt and pepper, to taste

1 large onion, diced small
3 Tb. olive oil
4 baking potatoes, peeled, diced medium
3 large eggs, lightly beaten
1 tsp. each, ground coriander, black pepper, and fennel seed
Salt, to taste
1 cup finely chopped toasted almonds
1 cup fine bread crumbs
1 cup all-purpose flour
2 large eggs, lightly beaten
Vegetable oil, for cooking

¾ pound smoked salmon, sliced thin
1 cup crème fraîche or sour cream
1½ Tb. minced fresh dill
Fresh dill sprigs, for garnish

Combine the tomatoes, olive oil, vodka, salt, and pepper in a nonreactive bowl. Taste and adjust the seasoning. Set the mixture aside at room temperature.

Cook the onion in the olive oil over moderate heat until the onion is transparent. Set aside.

Cook the potatoes in salted boiling water until very tender when pierced with a fork. Drain and cool. Do not run water over the potatoes. When they are cool enough to handle, pass through a ricer or use the large side of a grater. Add the sautéed onions, eggs, spices, and salt; mix well. Taste and adjust the seasoning. Cover and refrigerate the mixture for at least 1 hour.

When the potatoes are cold, remove them from the refrigerator and form into patties about ¾ inch thick and 2½ inches in diameter. Combine the almonds and bread crumbs. Dust each patty with flour, dip into the eggs, covering and coating the entire patty including the edges, with the almond-bread crumb mixture. Refrigerate the patties as you prepare them.

Heat a thin layer of vegetable oil in a large nonstick skillet. When the oil is hot, but not smoking, add the patties in batches, and cook over low heat until golden brown on one side. Carefully flip the cakes and cook until the second side is golden brown. Keep the potato cakes in a warm oven while you cook the remaining cakes.

Combine the crème fraîche and dill.

Spoon some of the Tomato Concasse onto each of 6 plates, place 2 or 3 potato cakes on each plate, cover with slices of smoked salmon, drizzle with crème fraîche, and garnish with a sprig of dill. Serve immediately.

Makes 6 servings.

Two-Pepper Chicken Salad with Pumpkin Seeds and Chipotle Mayonnaise on Corn Bread

This spicy and colorful chicken salad is a welcome alternative to the classic version. Pumpkin seeds add extra crunch.

Place the chicken, wine, stock, bay leaves, and black peppercorns in a large pot. Bring to a boil, reduce the heat, and simmer for about 25 minutes or until the chicken is springy to the touch and white all the way through. Remove from the liquid. When the chicken is cool enough to handle, remove the meat from the bones, taking care to remove all fat, tendons, and cartilage. Cut the meat into bite-size pieces. Place in a large bowl and refrigerate.

Combine the mayonnaise, chipotle pepper, garlic, lime juice, and spices; mix well. Set aside.

To the chicken, add the red and green peppers, onion, and cilantro. Add all but 6 tablespoons of the mayonnaise and mix well. Season with salt and pepper. Add the pumpkin seeds and mix.

Cut the corn bread into 6 pieces. Lightly spread each piece with the remaining mayonnaise. Cover with lettuce leaves and top with a slice of tomato. Spoon the salad over each tomato. Garnish with a sprig of cilantro.

Makes 6 servings.

COOK'S NOTE:

Chipotle peppers, which are smoked and marinated jalapeño peppers, can be found in small cans in Latin-American food shops. The peppers are very hot, but have a wonderful smoky intense flavor. Taste them with caution, but do taste; each can of peppers can have a different heat intensity.

4 whole chicken breasts
1 cup white wine
3 cups chicken stock
3 bay leaves
1 Tb. black peppercorns

CHIPOTLE
  MAYONNAISE
1¼ cups Mayonnaise
  (see page 12)
1 to 2 Tb. chipotle
  peppers, puréed
  (see COOK'S NOTE)
2 cloves garlic, minced
2 Tb. fresh lime juice
2 tsp. each, ground
  coriander and cumin
1 tsp. oregano

1 small red pepper, diced
  small
1 small green pepper,
  diced small
1 small red onion, diced
  small
⅓ cup chopped cilantro
Salt and pepper, to taste
⅔ cup toasted pumpkin
  seeds

1 recipe Corn Bread
  (see page 29)
12 lettuce leaves, trimmed
  to fit bread
6 slices tomato
Cilantro sprigs, for
  garnish

Noodle Pancake with Grilled Prawn Salad

*A*sian *spices combined with mayonnaise make this salad unique. The crispy noodle pancakes and spicy prawn salad are a sophisticated and pleasing team.*

MARINADE
½ cup olive oil
⅓ cup toasted sesame oil
¼ cup teriyaki sauce
2 Tb. sherry vinegar
1 2-inch piece fresh
   ginger, peeled and
   minced
2 cloves garlic, minced

1 pound prawns, peeled

NOODLE PANCAKES
½ pound very thin egg
   noodles, such as
   spaghettini
½ cup hoisin sauce
1 small yellow onion,
   sliced thin
1 tsp. red pepper flakes
2 large eggs, lightly
   beaten
Salt and pepper, to taste
Vegetable oil, for cooking

Combine the marinade ingredients; mix well. Place the prawns in a heavy plastic bag and pour the marinade over them. Seal the bag and marinate overnight in the refrigerator or for 2½ hours at room temperature.

Meanwhile, prepare the noodle pancake. Cook the noodles in salted boiling water until al dente. Do not overcook. Drain and allow the noodles to cool to room temperature. Place them in a large bowl. Add the hoisin sauce, onion, red pepper flakes, eggs, salt, and pepper; mix well. Heat about ½ inch of vegetable oil in a 12-inch skillet. When the oil is hot, but not smoking, add the noodles and spread them to the sides of the pan, making an even layer. Cook the noodles over low heat until golden brown on one side. To flip them, invert the pancake onto a large plate and slide back into the pan, uncooked side down. Cook until the second side is golden brown. Set aside.

Prepare a charcoal grill.

When the coals are hot, place the prawns on the grill and cook until the shells are opaque, 2 to 3 minutes, depending on the size of the prawns. Remove from the grill. When the prawns are cool enough to handle, chop into bite-size pieces and set aside.

In a large bowl, combine the miso, mayonnaise, soy sauce, vinegar, garlic, cilantro, spices, salt, and pepper; mix well. Add the cucumber and radishes; mix well. Add the chopped prawns. Taste and adjust the seasoning.

Cut the noodle pancake into 6 wedges and cover each wedge with a lettuce leaf. Spoon some salad onto the lettuce and garnish with a sprig of cilantro.

Makes 6 servings.

⅓ cup red miso
1 cup Mayonnaise
   (see page 12)
2 Tb. soy sauce
1 Tb. sherry vinegar
2 cloves garlic, minced
⅓ cup chopped cilantro
½ tsp. each, ground
   cumin, coriander, and
   turmeric
Pinch each, nutmeg,
   mace, and cinnamon
Salt and pepper, to taste
½ English cucumber,
   peeled, seeded, and
   diced small
6 radishes, sliced thin
6 lettuce leaves, trimmed
   to fit wedges
Cilantro sprigs, for
   garnish

Apricot Cream Cheese and Pears on Maple-Pecan Bread

*A*n *easy-to-prepare breakfast sandwich. The sliced pears make a stunning image, almost like wings. Any dried fruit could be used in the cream cheese.*

Combine the cream cheese and apricots. Spread the mixture on the 6 slices of bread. Stand a line of sliced pears on their edges in the cream cheese.

Makes 6 servings.

½ pound natural cream
   cheese, softened
⅓ cup dried apricots,
   chopped fine

6 slices Maple-Pecan
   Bread (see page 31)
3 firm pears, halved,
   seeded, and sliced thin

Danish Blue Cheese with Tomato and Fried Onions on Pumpernickel

*T*he aroma of onions frying in olive oil lures people into the kitchen. This recipe was inspired by traditional Danish sandwiches. If you like blue cheese and fried onions, you will love this version.

½ pound Danish blue
   cheese, softened
⅓ pound natural cream
   cheese, softened
⅓ cup currants
½ tsp. anise seed
Black pepper, to taste
2 Tb. olive oil
2 Tb. unsalted butter
3 medium yellow onions,
   sliced medium

6 thick slices
   pumpernickel, toasted
12 slices tomato
6 sprigs flat leaf parsley,
   for garnish

Combine the blue cheese, cream cheese, currants, and anise seed in a bowl; mix well. Season with pepper.

Heat the oil and butter in a large skillet. When the butter has melted, add the onions and cook over high heat for 5 to 7 minutes, stirring frequently. When the onions are golden brown, reduce the heat and keep them warm.

Spread each slice of bread with the cheese mixture and place 2 slices of tomato on top. Cover those with onions and garnish with sprigs of parsley. Serve immediately.

Makes 6 servings.

Roast Pork with Avocado-Jicama Salsa on Corn Tortillas

*T*ender and peppery, the pork makes a flavorful backdrop for the lighter taste of the salsa.

Preheat oven to 425° F.

Rub the pork with salt, pepper, and garlic. Place on a rack in a lightly greased roasting pan. Place in the oven and roast the meat 30–35 minutes. Remove from the oven and let rest for 5 minutes. When the meat is cool enough to handle, slice thin.

Combine the jicama, garlic, onion, tomatoes, jalapeño peppers, and cilantro in a large nonreactive bowl; mix well. Season with salt and pepper. Add the avocados and lime juice and stir carefully so as not to break the avocados.

Put cheese on each tortilla. Place a thin layer of oil in a large skillet or on a griddle. Add the tortillas and cook over low heat until the cheese just starts to melt. Cover each tortilla with meat. Garnish with avocado-jicama salsa. Serve immediately.

Makes 6 servings.

2 pounds pork tenderloin
Salt and black pepper
8 cloves garlic, minced
½ cup jicama, diced small (see COOK'S NOTE)
1 clove garlic, minced
1 small onion, diced small
2 small tomatoes, diced small
3 jalapeño peppers, minced
¼ cup chopped cilantro
Salt and pepper, to taste
2 avocados, peeled, pitted, and diced small
Juice of 2 limes

¾ pound Monterey Jack cheese, grated
6 or 12 Corn Tortillas, preferably homemade (see page 35)
Vegetable oil, for cooking

COOK'S NOTE:

If jicama is not available, you may substitute a firm apple.

Onion-Rye Bagels with Gravlax and Caper Cream Cheese

*C**hoose the freshest salmon for the gravlax. An elegant and traditional morning sandwich.*

GRAVLAX

1½ pounds fresh salmon, cleaned and boned

½ bunch fresh dill

3 Tb. kosher salt

2 Tb. sugar

2 Tb. freshly cracked pink peppercorns

CAPER CREAM CHEESE

1 pound natural cream cheese, softened

3 Tb. capers

1 Tb. lemon zest

Black pepper

6 Onion-Rye Bagels, halved (see page 26)

Dill sprigs, for garnish

Wash the salmon under cold water; pat dry. Place half the fish skin side down in a deep glass, stainless steel, or enamel baking dish. Place the dill on the fish. Combine the salt, sugar, and peppercorns in a small bowl and sprinkle over the fish. Top with the remaining fish, skin side up. Cover with aluminum foil and set a flat object larger than the fish on top of it. Place some heavy weights on the flat object. Weight the fish for 2 to 3 days. Every 12 hours, baste the fish with the accumulated juices, separating the halves a little to baste the inside of the salmon.

Remove the salmon and scrape away the dill and all the remaining seasonings. Pat the fish dry.

Slice into very thin pieces, removing the skin as you go. Set aside.

Combine the caper cream cheese ingredients, taste, and adjust the seasoning.

Spread the cream cheese on the cut sides of the bagels and top with thin slices of gravlax. Garnish with a sprig of dill.

Makes 6 servings.

Index